MW00453784

America
Say Jesus

David Allbritton

insight
PUBLISHING GROUP
Tulsa, Oklahoma

AMERICA SAY JESUS
© 2005 by David Allbritton

Published by Insight Publishing Group
8801 S. Yale, Suite 410
Tulsa, OK 74137
918-493-1718

All rights reserved. No part of this book may be reproduced or transmitted in any form or by any means, electronic or mechanical, including photocopying and recording, or by an information storage and retrieval system, without permission in writing from the author.

Scripture quotations are taken from the King James Version of the Holy Bible.

ISBN 1-932503-37-4
Library of Congress catalog card number: 2004111615

Printed in the United States of America

Dedication

I would like to dedicate this book to my mom and dad. My parents have always been such a blessing to my sister, Sharon and I. They have always shown us such love and have helped guide us through difficult times.

Sharon and I are also very proud and thankful to God for their success. Every church they ever pastored more than tripled in size. Their last church, First Family Church of Dallas, Texas, was birthed by Mom & Dad. They oversaw the growth of the church from twenty-nine people to over four thousand members. Today, First Family Church continues to grow and win souls under the direction of Dr. Jon and Toni Ogle.

Today, my wife, Linda and I continue to be amazed at my parents' strength and strong faith in God. They have constantly encouraged us through difficult times and have celebrated with us in our victories.

We all love my parents, Pastor Bert and Jean Allbritton. Dad is still preaching and souls continue to be saved.

We love you Mom and Dad!

Quotes from Our Founding Fathers

John Jay, First Chief Justice of the United States Supreme Court, said this in 1816, "Providence has given to our people the choice of their rulers and it is the duty, as well as the privilege and interest of our Christian nation to select and prefer Christians for their rulers."

The U.S. Supreme Court—1892, "Our Laws and our institutions are necessarily based upon the teachings of the Redeemer of mankind. It is impossible that it should be otherwise and in this sense and to this extent our civilization and our institution are emphatically Christian."

One of our leading Founding Fathers and noted statesman, Noah Webster, proclaimed, "No truth is more evident to my mind than that the Christian religion must be the basis of any government intended to secure the rights and privileges of a free people."

President Hoover made one of the boldest statements for Christianity during his generation. President Hoover emphatically explained, "The whole inspiration of our civilization springs from the teachings of Christ and the lessons of the prophets. To read the Bible for these fundamentals is a necessity of American life."

In 1954, Chief Justice Earl Warren said, "I believe no one can read the history of our country without realizing that the good book and the Spirit of the Savior from the beginning has been our guiding geniuses... Whether we look to the first Charter of Virginia or the Charter of New England or the Charter of Massachusetts Bay or to the Fundamental Orders of Connecticut... the same objective is present: a Christian land governed by Christian principles."

President Andrew Johnson summed up the feeling of millions of Americans when he boldly exhorted, "Let us look forward to the time when we can take the flag of our country and nail it below the Cross, and there let it wave as it waved in the olden times, and let us gather around it and inscribe for our motto: 'Liberty and Union, one and inseparable, now and forever,' and exclaim, **Christ first, our country next!**"

Theodore Roosevelt, our twenty-sixth American President said, "the United States was founded on the principle of Christianity." He also noted, "Every thinking man, when he thinks, realizes that the teachings of the Bible are so interwoven and entwined with our whole civic and social life that it would be literally—I do not mean figuratively, but literally—impossible for us to figure what that loss would be if these teachings were removed. We would lose all the standards by which we now judge both public and private morals; all the standards towards which we, with more or less resolution, strive to raise ourselves."

And President John Adams said, "The highest story of the American Revolution is this: it connected in one indissoluble bond the principles of civil government with the principles of Christianity."

President Andrew Jackson explained his love for Christ and His dependence on God in this letter to his son in 1834, "I nightly offer up my prayers to the throne of grace for the health and safety of you all, and that we ought all to rely with confidence on the promises of our dear Redeemer, and give Him our hearts. This is all he requires and all that we can do, and if we sincerely do this, we are sure of salvation through his atonement."

And again, in another letter in 1835, President Jackson showed his deep faith in Jesus Christ, "All who profess Christianity believe in a Savior, and that by and through Him we must be saved."

Patrick Henry made it clear, "It cannot be emphasized too strongly or too often that this great country was founded not by religionists, but by Christians; not on religions, but on the gospel of Jesus Christ. For this very reason, people of other faiths have been afforded asylum, prosperity and freedom to worship here."

Former President James Madison warned our generation, "We have staked the whole future of American civilization not on the power of government, far from it. We have staked the future of all of our political institutions upon the capacity of each and all of us to govern ourselves according to the Ten Commandments of God."

Contents

Foreword
By Thaddeus Freeman, Attorney-at-Law

When someone asks what I do, I am fond of saying, "I'm a believer in Jesus; being an attorney is just what I do making a living." As a believer, I often ask the Holy Spirit in my quiet time what to pray for. In early 2002, the "sense" coming back was to pray for the name of Jesus to be used in public by believers in office. For three months I lifted up this burden to the Lord. I would often say that there's no legal reason for politicians not to profess Jesus' name.

In the spring of that year, I was listening to a local Christian talk radio show, when a preacher came on with a new ministry. He not only focused on the name of Jesus, but wanted politicians and bureaucrats to lift up the name in public, along with all Americans. His heart's desire was to bring hundreds of millions to Christ in America as a continuation of the millions he brought to Christ in Africa and other continents of the world.

It took only a half-minute to decide to go to this preacher's next soul winning seminar. There, I met David Allbritton for the first time. Our introduction was short, but I was able to introduce myself, give him a card, and say I did not know exactly why I was there, but if he needed anything to please let me know.

Since that meeting, I have had the privilege of being in on the ground floor of David's outreach to follow God's direction in bringing the name of Jesus to the forefront of the inner workings of our culture, politics, and families. Better still, David is a soul-winner and is believing God for marshalling the Christians around the country to turn this nation back to, "One nation, under Jesus Christ."

I cannot encourage you enough to take the time to read how God has anointed David to help bring our nation out of its demoralizing downward spiral. In the pages that follow, the skeptic will be prompted to seek out Jesus. At the very least, he or she will want to find out more about Him. The new believer will know, through Bible verses and the Holy Spirit's prompting, why the name of Jesus is so powerful: a power that God wants His people to have and call upon. And finally, the seasoned believer will discover new insights and factual bases on why it is so critically important for God not to lift His hand of favor and protection from our country, and what part all three will play in keeping His anointing on us. In the end, we're all going somewhere. David's heart and hence, God's way of using David, is that we join Him in the life to come. Please continue reading how each of us has a role to play in, "The Great Commission" of winning souls to Christ and keeping God's favor on our nation.

A Testimony from Mike Nelson
of Red Rock Energy Partners

On September 14, 1976, my wife and I met Jesus in our home in Garland, Texas, when a Baptist Pastor and his wife came for a visit. At the time, my wife was a good Catholic girl who did not know Jesus, and I was a twenty-seven-year-old guy that walked the aisle as a young boy, but never lived for Jesus. We joined the church that he pastored and stayed there for about two years. In 1978, we moved on to a charismatic church, and there we met the Holy Spirit, and our lives have not been the same since.

In 1979, I was driving down Miller Road in Dallas, Texas, and in front of Slaughter Lumber Company, the Holy Spirit spoke to me in a clear voice and said, "I am going to make you a financier of the Gospel." At that time, the most money that I had made in one year was around $30,000. But I knew that what He had spoken, if I was willing, would come to pass. In 1981, I got into the oil and gas business. I started my first company in 1982 with three other partners. In 1986, at Church of the Rock in Rockwall, Texas, a prophet name Dick Mills prophesied over me out of Luke 5. He said that, as Peter and Andrew had to call to shore to their partners James and John to come and help them with the great catch of fish, I too would have to call to my partners to help me with the great catch of finances that He was going to give me. Then in 1990, at the same church, I met Dale Gentry and my life radically changed. Dale prophesied for about twenty minutes over my wife and me and gave us some powerful words from the Lord. Many have come to pass and some were confirming words of what I already knew. Since then, I have received many words from the Lord. Most of them are centered on the area of finance and business.

My life was a roller coaster for much of the time until 1999, when I started directing operations for a small independent company that I had actually funded the start-up and at one time owned 50 percent of the stock. After I had given my half of the stock back, the company drilled a successful well in East Texas and shortly later, contacted me about helping them develop the prospect. Suddenly, I found myself working for the very man that once worked for me and whom I had taught the oil and gas business to. It's funny how God does things. Everything does not always, or should I say seldom does He do things in a manner that we expect. During these two years, I often thought of Jacob working for Laban or Joseph and his many plights as he went from the pit to Potiphar's house to the Palace. When God is in control, we need to learn to relax and not lean to our own understanding. He takes us places we've never been, causes us to do things we've never done, and connects us to people we've never met and on and on.

In 2001, just after September 11, my partner, Dan Griffin and I started Red Rock Energy Partners, Ltd. Dan is a young man who has fallen in love with Jesus and possesses great business skills. His heart is to wake up the Gatekeepers for the Kingdom of God. The Lord gave the name to Dan. Red is for the blood of Jesus and Rock is the Christ. He blessed us with a rapid start and in short order, we had seven producing wells in Western Louisiana and a substantial income. Everything about this was a miracle after a miracle. He told us that He would show us where to drill. He has since shown us several places to drill. Our calling is to make money for the Kingdom of God and our goal is to give 90 percent of what we earn back into the Kingdom. We currently partner with four ministries that God put on our hearts. One is David Allbritton, whom I believe God has chosen for this hour to lead this nation back to Jesus. We have become a nation much like the Greeks in Athens when Paul visited the first time, in that we, as a nation, worship many gods. Our God is a jealous God and there are not many routes to heaven, as many believe. Only through Jesus Christ can one be saved and this is the mandate God has given David Allbritton to wake up America and say Jesus is our God and there is no other.

When the Lord spoke to me in my prayer closet to start supporting David, I had not even spoken to him or met him. After a long period of time, David called me and asked, "Who are you?" Soon after that, David and his lovely wife, Linda, came to our home in Argyle, Texas, and it was there that the

Lord really bonded us. We sat at our kitchen table and the presence of the Lord was as tangible as I have ever experienced as David gave testimony after testimony of what God had done in his life. At one time, David said, "I don't know why God chose me for this task," and I laughed out loud, because it was so apparent to me why God would choose him. He is radical for the gospel like none I have met. His testimonies are radical. Everything about him is radical and it will take someone radical for the gospel to lead in this task that I believe holds this nation's very survival in its outcome. If ever one desired to plant seeds in a fertile soil for the Kingdom's sake, here is the opportunity. When we stand before Jesus at the Judgment Seat of Christ to receive our rewards for what we've done while on this earth, I believe that America Say Jesus will be a hot topic.

Introduction

About four months after the tragic day of September 11, Linda and I found ourselves ministering in Ethiopia. It was a joy to see over 1.1 million people give their lives to Jesus Christ. At that time, I thought we would spend most of our lives in Africa conducting citywide crusades.

However, when we came home, I was overwhelmed by the power of the Holy Spirit. God gave me such a burden for America that I would often cry throughout the night.

Under the direction of the Holy Spirit, we moved from Dallas, Texas to Florida. Within a few short months, the Lord told us to start a new church called "America's Church." And a short time later, God told me to launch the "America Say Jesus" national ministry and caravan.

At first, none of it made any sense. After all, we had just resigned a four thousand member church in Dallas, Texas to conduct city wide crusades in Africa. Plus, Dallas was our financial base, and international evangelism was our main calling.

For the next eighteen months, Linda and I trusted God just to pay our bills. Each month, God supernaturally met our needs.

During this difficult time, my heart was breaking over the ungodliness of our nation. Many of my sermons were soaked with tears. I was broken because our sinful nation was trying to deny Jesus Christ. Liberal politicians and judges were systematically trying to get Jesus out of our culture. And even some Christian ministers were refusing to pray in the name of Jesus.

One day God spoke to me and said, "America Say Jesus." God went on and explained what He wanted me to do.

Since that day, God has led Linda and I, and our three children step by step. We tried to sell our motor coach, but God wouldn't go for it. Instead, the Lord told me to paint "America Say Jesus" on it and drive that motor coach to the West Coast and back and throughout America. God told me to lead a national caravan, to preach at the courthouses, capitols, and to conduct citywide crusades in the largest stadiums in America to lift up the name of Jesus. He told me to get Christians everywhere to say "Jesus" and He instructed me to launch a petition to our President to publicly say the name of Jesus Christ. He also told me to write this manuscript.

As you read this book, Linda, the family and I are somewhere in America preaching the gospel of Jesus Christ. Please pray with us for the name of Jesus to be lifted up and for souls to be saved.

The journey we're on is a faith journey for Jesus. Each day, each week, and each month we trust God to meet the needs of this ministry. Someday, I hope we can have a surplus, so we can invest more into the kingdom of God, and win even more souls to Christ.

Whatever happens, we will continue to listen to God's voice and to follow in the steps of Jesus.

The Lord told me that America must define her God. America's God is not Buddha or Muhammad, but His name is Jesus Christ. Many in our nation are promoting a pluralistic god, but nevertheless the only true God is Jesus Christ. Jesus is God the Son and the Son of God. Jesus said, "If I be lifted up, I will draw all men unto me."

Demons tremble at the name of Jesus. Let's make the devil shake all over. Let's talk about Jesus, preach Jesus, and sing Jesus. Let's turn America back to Jesus Christ.

Together we can do it for Christ's sake and future generations!

Your friend,
David Allbritton

P.S. Please check out our Web site at wincityonline.org or call our ministry at 1-888-30-JESUS for our caravan schedule and/or crusade schedule.

ONE

The Attack Against Jesus and What Our Founding Fathers Really Believed!

Our country is under attack! The United States of America is in deep trouble. Our beloved country is at war at home and abroad.

The war against Islamic terrorists is raging throughout the world, and here at home secular humanists are determined to get God out of our American culture.

Liberal judges and lawmakers are systematically undermining and destroying our Christian heritage. The Ten Commandments and Nativity scenes are being removed while the homosexual agenda is being promoted.

The haters of God cannot stand the name of Jesus. Today it is politically incorrect to say the name that is above every name. Many politicians and most liberal theologians are even anti-Christ.

Just a few years ago, adultery was called a sin and homosexuality was called a perversion. However, today, our nation has lost its moral soul and is floundering in a cesspool of iniquity. Something must be done or we may lose our nation forever.

Since September 11, Americans are praying again, and God is now popular. School signs, banks, and businesses of all kinds boldly proclaim, "God bless America." National and local prayer meetings express belief in God. Yet something, Someone's Name, (the Name that is above <u>Every</u> name) is missing.

Mysteriously, the name of Jesus isn't mentioned. Allah and Mohammed are given respect, as is Buddha and the gods of Hinduism. Eastern gurus are allowed to pray in the name of their gods, and even witches, Satanists, and various cultic beliefs are honored and given respect.

It seems as though America is very godly. Even our congressmen gathered on steps of the Capitol and sang "God Bless America." Yet, to what God is America praying?

Americans want God to bless the United States and to protect her from her enemies. Yet, how can our country expect God's favor when she is serving other gods and is ashamed of the Lord Jesus Christ?

According to the Bible, it's only through Jesus Christ that a person can find salvation and have favor with God (2 Corinthians 5:17-21). Acts 4:12 reads, "Neither is there salvation in any other; for there is no other name under heaven given among men whereby we must be saved." The apostle Paul wrote, "that at the name of Jesus every knee shall bow and every tongue confess that Jesus Christ is Lord, to the glory of God the Father" (Philippians 2:10-11).

One of the world's top military leaders and respected battle-field innovators had a conversion on his deathbed. Napoleon wrote, "I know men and I tell you Jesus Christ is not a man. Superficial minds see a resemblance between Christ and the founders of empires, and the gods of other religions. That resemblance does not exist. There is between Christianity and whatever other religions the distance of infinity ... everything in Christ astonishes me. I search in vain in history to find similar to Jesus Christ or anything, which can approach the gospel. Neither history, nor humanity, nor the ages, nor nature, offer me anything with which I am able to compare it or to explain it."

At first, I was so excited to hear God on the lips of so many Americans and to see Him back in our lives, culture and politics. But I soon discovered some of Satan's diabolical schemes. The devil is using our secular media and government to promote a pluralistic god and an anti-Christ spirit in our nation.

This is exactly what happened in the book of Acts. The Church of Jesus Christ was growing rapidly and the devil's main tactic was to make it illegal to preach, teach, or even speak the name of Jesus. We read one of these threats in Acts 4:18, "And they called them and commanded them not to speak at all or teach in the name of Jesus."

We have no such law in the United States, but many Americans refuse to speak the name of Jesus and thousands more oppose the name of Christ.

When President George W. Bush mentioned the name of Jesus during a pre-election debate, the national media attacked him unmercifully. Perhaps this is one of the reasons why most presidents in office (including President Bush) refuse to say Jesus in any public forum (unless at a Christian gathering).

After Rev. Franklin Graham prayed in the name of Jesus during the inaugural, many in the media went ballistic. Anger was expressed from coast to coast. The famous attorney for O.J. Simpson, Allan Dershowitz, said, "The very first act of the new Bush administration was to have a Protestant Evangelical minister officially dedicate the inauguration to Jesus Christ, who he declared to be 'our Savior', invoking 'the Father, the Son, the Lord Jesus Christ and the Holy Spirit.' Billy Graham's son, the man selected by George W. Bush to bless his presidency, excluded the tens of millions of Americans who are Muslims, Jews, Buddhists, Shintoists, Unitarians, Agnostics and Atheists from his blessing by his particularistic and parochial language. It is permissible in the United States to reject any particular theology. Indeed that is part of our glorious diversity. What is not acceptable is for the presidential inauguration to exclude millions of citizens from its opening ceremony by dedicating it to a particular religious 'savior'. If Bush wants all Americans to accept him as their president, he made an inauspicious beginning by sandwiching his unity speech between two divisive, sectarian and inappropriate prayers."

Evidently, our first President, George Washington didn't feel that way, for he constantly prayed in Jesus' name. In his prayer book, *Hours In Prayer*, President Washington prayed:

"Let the world, oh Lord, be filled with the knowledge of thee and thy Son, Jesus Christ. Wash away my sins in the immaculate blood of the Lamb and purge my heart by the Holy Spirit. Daily frame me more and more into the likeness of thy Son Jesus Christ."

As a matter of fact, fifty-two of the fifty-five framers of our Constitution were Christians. Of the fifteen thousand writings of our founding fathers, about 94 percent of all their quotes were cited from the Bible. Former President Andrew Jackson regarding the Bible said, "That book sir, is the rock upon which our republic rests."

Of the first 108 Universities, 106 were Christian. In 1636, the rules and precepts of Harvard read: " Let every student be plainly instructed, and earnestly pressed to consider well, the main end of his life and studies is to know God and Jesus Christ which is eternal life, John 17:3, and therefore to lay Christ in the bottom as the only foundation of all sound knowledge and learning."

In 1692, the Charter for the College of William and Mary expressed its purpose "That the Christian faith may be propagated... to the glory of God."

Another institution of higher learning said in 1701, "Our university was founded to propagate in the wilderness the blessed reformed, Protestant religion, with a goal that every student shall consider the main end of his study to wit to know God and Jesus Christ and answerably to lead a Godly, sober life." So were the words penned by the leaders at Yale College.

As a matter of fact, eighty-seven of the signers of the Declaration of Independence attended Princeton. Its first President declared, "Cursed be all learning that is contrary to the cross of Christ." Nearly all the College presidents up to the early 1900s were clergymen.

By the time of the American Revolution, 99.8 percent of the colonists claimed to be believers in Christ. The famous cry of the colonists was "No king, but King Jesus."

In David Limbaugh's book *Persecution*, he vividly shows the anti-Christ movement that is sweeping America. This great attorney and well-known nationally syndicated columnist writes:

"Prayers in the name of Jesus before City Council meetings are now being challenged throughout the land." Mr. Limbaugh went on and explained, "At a November 1999 city council meeting in Burbank, California, the minister ended his invocation prayer with 'in the name of Jesus Christ.' Someone in attendance was offended and filed a suit in the Supreme Court of Los Angeles to ban the practice. The court complied and the appellate court affirmed the ban in September 2002."

Mr. Limbaugh went on and explained how thirty-four cities began to re-evaluate their invocations. In Buena Park and La Palma, city officials asked clergy not to mention a particular deity in their prayers. In Fullerton, the city attorney directed that invocations could begin with "our heavenly Father" but could not end with references to "Jesus."

The book *Persecution* is a tremendous resource in proving the anti-Christ spirit that has determined to eliminate Jesus from the public domain. During Christmas, it is no longer politically correct to say "Merry Christmas." To be on the cutting edge and in with the intellectual crowd you should rather say "Happy Holidays."

Many in our nation seem to believe that America has always been anti-religious or at least pluralistic. Most citizens of the United States don't have a clue regarding the Christian heritage of our beloved country. From the very beginning, Christians have been the majority of this great nation. From the early Pilgrims and Puritans to every American settlement, Christians were not only the majority, but the laws of the land were based on the Christian religion.

By the time of the Revolution, nearly everyone was a Christian, most of which were evangelical Protestant. The well-known scholar M. E. Bradford (University of Dallas), who studies the religious backgrounds of the signers of the Declaration and the Constitution, concluded that the over-whelming majority of them were strong practicing Christians. Bradford found that fifty-two of the fifty-six signers of the Declaration were Trinitarian Christians. Similarly, of the fifty-five signers of the Constitution, fifty to fifty-two were orthodox Christians.

Without a doubt, this nation was founded by a Christian missionary, Christopher Columbus, and established by evangelical believers. Its entire system of government (and most of the free world) is based on the Word of God. From 1776 to the present hour, Christianity is the most powerful force for righteousness and family values.

As I have traveled into some forty-five nations of the world, most every country's news media describes America as a Christian nation. Islam countries hate us, because in their mind, we are a Christian country.

From the inception of our country, our presidents have often referred to America as a Christian country and often spoke of their own relationship with Jesus Christ. Former President Theodore Roosevelt once said, "After a week on perplexing problems it does so rest my soul to... come into the House of the Lord and to sing and mean it, 'Holy, Holy, Holy, Lord God Almighty'... (my) great joy and glory that, in occupying an exalted position in the nation, I am enabled to preach the practical moralities of the Bible to my fellow countrymen and to hold up Christ as the hope and Savior of the world."

President George Washington said this in a speech to the Delaware Indian chiefs: "You do well to wish to learn our arts and ways of life and above all, the religion of Jesus Christ... Congress will do everything they can to assist you in this wise intention." Washington also encouraged his troops "to live and act as becomes a Christian soldier."

President James Madison (the Father of the Constitution and our fourth President) wrote in the margins of his own Bible, "Believers who are in a state of grace, have need of the Word of God for their edification and building up therefore implies the possibility of falling." President Madison was also educated at Princeton under the Rev. John Witherspoon who wrote, "Cursed be all learning that is contrary to Christ."

Another strong advocate of the Constitution and one of the three authors of the Federalist papers, Alexander Hamilton, wrote, "I have carefully examined the evidences of the Christian religion, and if I was sitting as a juror upon its authenticity I would unhesitantly give my verdict in its favor. I can prove its truth as clearly as any proposition ever submitted to the mind of man."

John Adams said that this nation was founded on "the general principles of Christianity." Thomas Jefferson made it clear, "No nation has ever yet existed or been governed without religion. Nor can be. The Christian religion is the best religion that has ever been given to man and I as chief Magistrate of this nation am bound to give it the sanction of my example."

French historian Alexis d'eTocquevilli said, "For Americans the idea of Christianity and liberty are so completely mingled that it is almost impossible to get them to conceive of the one without the other." He reiterated, "there is no country in the world where the Christian religion retains a greater influence over the souls of man than in America."

The foundation of our great nation is based upon the Word of God, the belief in the Holy Trinity, and salvation only by Jesus Christ. Unless America turns back to the Bible and to Jesus Christ, God's judgment will fall on this ungodly, anti-Christ country. America's God must be defined, and His name is Jesus Christ.

By the mercies of God, I want to encourage and exhort you to say the name of Jesus, every day to every person you meet. And by all means, say it to the unbelievers and try to lead them to Christ.

Millions of Americans already testify of a changed life in Christ Jesus. That is why God laid it on my heart to launch a national movement called "America Say Jesus." We want Christians to lift up the name that is above every name. Jesus said, "If I be lifted up, I will draw all men unto me." Jesus said in John 14:6, "I am the Way, the Truth, and the Life: no man cometh unto the Father but by me."

May God help each of us to do something before it's too late. The time has come for America to say Jesus again. We believe it will spark a national spiritual awakening. Please help us turn America back to God.

Psalm 33:12, "Blessed is that nation whose God is the Lord."

Acts 8:5-8, "Then Philip went down to the city of Samaria and preached Christ unto them. And the people with one accord gave heed unto those things in which Philip spoke, hearing and seeing the miracle, which he did. For unclean spirits, crying with a loud voice came out of many that were possessed with them and many were taken with palsies and that were lame, were healed. **And there was Great Joy in that City."**

The Virginia colonists declared in Virginia's first Charter that their goal was to "spread the Christian religion to such people as yet live in darkness and miserable ignorance of the true knowledge and worship of God."

The Mayflower Compact says in part, "having under taken for the glory of God and for the advancement of the Christian faith."

Thomas Jefferson confessed, "I hold these teachings of Jesus as delivered by himself, to be the most pure, benevolent and sublime which have ever been preached to man."

George Washington said, "It is impossible to rightly govern the world without God and the Bible."

Abraham Lincoln said, "The great book (the Bible) is the best gift God has ever given to man."

William Lynch Phelps said" Western civilization is founded upon the Bible."

Charles Dickens—" The New Testament is the best book the world has ever known or will know."

Immanuel Kent—"The Bible is the greatest benefit which the human race has ever experienced."

Even the founder of our country, Christopher Columbus, claimed to be a missionary for Jesus Christ. He wrote, "Our Lord Jesus desired to perform a very obvious miracle in the voyage of the Indies. It was the Lord who put into my mind the fact that it would be possible to sail from here to the Indies. All who heard of my project rejected it with laughter, ridiculing me. There is no question that the inspiration was from the Holy Spirit, because He comforted me with rays of marvelous inspiration from Holy Scriptures... No one should fear to undertake any task in the name of our Savior, if it is just and if the intention is purely for His holy service."

Ladies and Gentlemen, simply put, America was founded by Christians to propagate the gospel of Christ to the ends of the earth. About 80 percent of the world's missionaries come from the United States of America.

Even today, our nation is saturated with Christian thought, ideology and Christian culture. The anti-Christ spirit has a long way to go to banish Christianity.

One man, who tried to get "Under God" out of the Pledge of Allegiance, was finally defeated by the U.S. Supreme Court. We have won many cases but have also lost some vitally important ones.

Recently, the American Civil Liberties Union won a case against the city of Los Angeles. A court ordered the removal of the cross from L.A.'s official logo. Other such attacks against Christianity continue in various parts of the country.

However, I would like to remind the American Civil Liberties Union of a few facts. America's founding fathers did not intend for there to be a separation of Church and State, as shown by the fact that all fifty states acknowledge God in their state constitution. For example, in 1776, the Virginia Bill of Rights XVI states, "Religion, or the duty which we owe our Creator... can be directed only by reason... and that it is the mutual duty of all to practice Christian forbearance, love and charity towards each other."

In 1820, Maine's Preamble reads, "We the people of Maine, acknowledging with grateful hearts the goodness of the Sovereign Ruler of the Universe in affording us an opportunity and imploring its aid and direction."

Just think, all fifty states acknowledged God in their constitution. Perhaps that's why William Penn stated, "Those people who will not be governed by God will be ruled by tyrants."

In 1853, a minority group of nonbelievers tried unsuccessfully to get the Congress to separate the government from Christian principles.

On March 27, 1854, The House Judiciary Committee gave its verdict. They wrote, "Had the people during the revolution had any suspicion of any attempt to war against Christianity, that revolution would have been strangled in its cradle."

The United States Senate also made a bold declaration regarding Christianity in America. The report said, "At the time of the adoption of the Constitution and the Amendments, the universal sentiment was that Christianity should be encouraged, but not any one sect. **In this age there can be no substitute for Christianity. That was the religion of the Founders of the Republic and they expected it remain the religion of their descendants**."

And they also reiterated their beliefs with the unmistakable statement regarding the place of Christianity in our country and government. "**The great, vital and conservative element in our system is the belief of our people in the pure doctrines and the divine truth of the gospel of Jesus Christ**."

Ladies and Gentlemen, Christianity is not only in place and ingrained throughout American history, but its impact can be seen via Bible verses etc.... throughout the Federal buildings and on various monuments in Washington, D.C. Even the Supreme Court has the Ten Commandments engraved on the walls and even on their two large oak doors that lead to the chamber.

Not only do you see Christianity and Bible verses displayed visibly throughout Washington, but it can also be seen and heard each opening session of Congress. Since 1777, a paid clergyman (paid by American tax dollars) opens each session in prayer.

Former President John Quincy Adams wrote, "The highest glory of the American Revolution was this: that it tied together in one indissoluble bond, the principles of civil government with the principles of Christianity."

President Thomas Jefferson explained, "The reason Christianity is the best friend of government is because it is the only religion in the world that deals with the heart."

These men believed so strongly in the God of the Bible that certain requirements were laid down for everyone holding an office. Most public officials had to make a public vow similar to the following that comes from the Delaware Constitution of 1776. It reads, "Everyone appointed to public office must say: 'I do profess faith in God the Father and in the Lord Jesus Christ his only Son, and in the Holy Ghost, one God and blessed forevermore: and I do acknowledge the Holy Scriptures of the Old & New Testaments to be given by divine inspiration."

Liberals in our country are trying to rewrite history and reinvent the wheel that would eliminate all moral law, its absolutes, and would try to banish the name of Jesus Christ. If they were to ever have their way, America would become a modern Sodom and Gomorrah and this great nation would eventually self-destruct.

I believe if our Founding Fathers were alive today, they would do everything they could to lift up the name of Jesus and to reestablish Christianity as the cornerstone of this nation.

In March of 1863, when President Abraham Lincoln was proclaiming a national day of prayer, he boldly witnessed for the God of the Bible and emphasized the need for the American people to repent of their sins:

> It is the duty of nations as well as of men to own their dependence upon the overruling power of God, to confess their sins and transgressions in humble sorrow... and to recognize the sublime truth, announced in the Holy Scriptures and proven by all history: that those nations only are blessed whose God is the Lord. We have been the recipients of the choicest bounties of Heaven. We have been preserved these many years amid prosperity. We have grown in numbers, wealth and power as no other nation has ever grown. But we have forgotten God. We have forgotten the gracious Hand, which preserved us in peace, and multiplied and enriched and strengthened us; and we have vainly imagined, in the deceitfulness of our hearts, that all these blessings were produced by some superior wisdom and virtue of our own. Intoxicated with unbroken success, we have become too self-sufficient to feel the necessity of redeeming and preserving grace, too proud to pray to the God that made us! It behooves us then to humble ourselves before the offended Power, to confess our national sins and to pray for clemency and forgiveness.

Congressman Daniel Webster warned, "If the power of the gospel is not felt throughout the length and breadth of the land, anarchy and misrule, degradation and misery, corruption and darkness will reign."

And isn't that precisely what is taking place in America? Since the Supreme Court overruled nearly two hundred years of law by outlawing school prayer in 1963, notice the moral decline.

Since 1963, violent crime has increased 544 percent and there has been over thirty million legalized abortions. In the first twelve years after taking prayer out of the classroom, sexually transmitted diseases increased by 226 percent. After the 1963 ruling, divorce increased 300 percent each year for the next fifteen years.

Since taking prayer out of the classroom, girls between the ages of ten to fourteen are experiencing an incredibly high rate of pregnancy. Pregnancies in this age group since 1963 are up 553 percent.

Since 1963, unmarried people living together is up 353 percent. Illegal drugs and alcohol are staggering habits for millions of Americans and are an overwhelming health care problem! And needless to say, the education system of America has deteriorated to the point that we have murder and rape in schools throughout America. In 2003, there were over 350 murders at our secular schools.

And President George Washington summed it up by saying, "Reason and experience both forbid us to expect that national morality can prevail in exclusion of religious principle."

Most of these great men of God, not only followed the Bible, but they also had a deep devotion for Jesus Christ. Even to their deathbed, these men proclaimed Jesus as their Savior.

On his deathbed, Alexander Hamilton said, "I have a tender reliance on the mercy of the Almighty, through the merits of the Lord Jesus Christ. I am a sinner, I look to Him for mercy."

Patrick Henry who proclaimed, "Give me liberty or give me death" made this statement before seeing Jesus, "This is all the inheritance I give to my dear family—Jesus Christ will make them rich indeed."

Another signer of the Constitution, Samuel Adams said, "First of all, I resign my soul to the Almighty Being who gave it... relying on the merits of Jesus Christ for the pardon of my sins."

And another signer of the constitution, Charles Carroll wrote, "On the mercy of my Redeemer, I rely for salvation and His merits; not on the works I have done in obedience to His precept."

Yes, our Founding Fathers were really determined to stand up for Christianity. Likewise, I have "set my face like a flint" to turn our nation back to Jesus Christ. I refuse to bow my knee to the worldly philosophy of situation ethics. On every occasion, regardless of the venue, I am determined to speak the name of Jesus and to witness to sinners. I refuse to deny the name that is above every name. I owe it to God, to Jesus and to the Holy Spirit, to preach His name to the ends of the earth. I owe it to my countrymen and to future generations to stand up for Biblical morality. And as an American, I feel a divine obligation to defend the purposes and the national design that our Founding Fathers had in mind for the United States of America.

We must never let the anti-Christ spirit of this nation twist the words or change the Christian foundation of this country. Our Constitution was written and framed by men who loved Jesus Christ.

Jesus died for the sins of mankind and rose again triumphantly. He is the only answer for this life and the life to come.

The following is my personal statement of faith. I hope all of us will make a new commitment to Jesus Christ. I pray each of you will be more determined than ever to say the name that is above every name. I hope everyone reading this book will make a commitment to reach our nation and the world for Jesus Christ.

I wrote my commitment on paper. Perhaps you may want to do the same thing, by expressing your commitment to God in your own words.

I wrote this early one morning after having a great time of prayer. The Holy Spirit's anointing was so evident as I penned these words:

My Statement of Faith

I want to dream big dreams and see the unseen. I want to risk in order to achieve. I do not choose indifference. The middle ground accommodates compromise. I choose instead to live under the mantle of God. To be a common Christian is to fail. I want to win souls to Christ, entire cities to Jesus and to turn America back to God. In my spirit is a "Fire Desire" to preach the unsearchable riches of God and to prophesy His message of redemption to the ends of the earth. Yes, I am only one man, yet I choose to stand up for the truth. I will not be intimidated by the lies of darkness, the threats of Satan, or the persecution of man. I choose to read my Bible, to pray in the Holy Spirit and to walk in victory. With God's help, I accept the challenge to win America. With a smile on my face and the love of God in my heart, I will turn America back to Jesus. By God's grace and help, I choose to rescue the perishing and to care for the dying. I ask you in Jesus name to help me win souls to Christ. Together we can win America and reap that supernatural harvest of lost souls!

Two

The Heart of America

What is the very heart and soul of America? The obvious answer is freedom. Most would agree that the United States represents liberty and justice for all. We are free to worship any god, go to any church, or hold the job of our preference. We have elected officials who represent the American people. There are no dictatorships or evil empires; Human rights are guaranteed under our Constitution.

The next questions must be: where does our freedom derive and from where has it emerged? What is the source, the foundation of our belief system?

Without a doubt, America is one nation under God. Not just any god, or a group of gods. America's heart and soul was explained over and over by our Founding Fathers. The God and only God of our nation is, was and will forever be Jesus Christ.

Christianity is the only religion in the history of the world that can change hearts. Any religion can reform the outside, but **ONLY** the God of Christianity can change the **INSIDE** of a person.

President George W. Bush was vilified, condemned, and ridiculed for an answer he gave during an exchange during the 2000 presidential debate. When asked, "Who is your favorite political philosopher?", George W. Bush answered, "Christ, because he changed my heart... When you turn your heart and your life over to Christ, when you accept Christ as Savior, it changes the heart and changes your life and that's what happened to me."

Yes, our future president was vehemently persecuted for telling the truth, not only about himself, but for millions of Americans who likewise have been changed by the power of Jesus Christ!

Following the 2002 Space Shuttle Columbia tragedy, President Bush said, "I've got a structure to my life where religion plays a role. I understand religion is a walk; it's a journey. And I fully recognize that I'm a sinner, just like you. That's why Christ died. He died for my sins and for your sins."

Was President Bush standing alone and denying the Founding Fathers by being so bold for Christ? Was he in some way out of step with our history, our people and with our current culture?

Well I'm sure the ACLU would want us to believe that most Americans are anti-Christ. But the fact remains, over 99 percent of our Founding Fathers were Christians, and even today, 80 to 85 percent of our nation's population is Christian.

When Mel Gibson tried to get various movie companies to produce *The Passion of the Christ*, he was abruptly scorned and rejected. So with his own money, Mr. Gibson produced one of the most successful films in the history of the world. Millions of Americans and millions more around the world fled to the theatres to watch the final hours of Christ.

Americans in particular couldn't stay away from the true story of our Lord's crucifixion. Mel Gibson even testified that the wounds of Jesus healed his wounds. People across America left the theatres in tears and many with changed lives. Jesus changed their hearts.

Yes, without a doubt, America's heart and soul are found in the gospel of Jesus Christ.

President Bush went on and explained how Christ changed his heart and how changed hearts can change society: "The seed from which my decision to run for President was sown by Billy Graham. He visited us for the weekend, and his words started a process of change in my heart. It was less his words than the power which he exuded, his friendly, loving manner, reflecting Jesus Christ so clearly. I was always a religious person, but gave my heart to Jesus Christ again on that weekend. I learned the power of prayer, and asked God for wisdom, patience and understanding. I am aware that faith can be wrongly interpreted in the political process. I want to live my faith, not boast of it. Faith changes lives. I know that, because faith changed my life. In order to change our culture, the heart, soul and consciousness must be transformed. The government can give money, but it cannot give hope in our hearts or a reason to live. But changed hearts change society."

To understand how Jesus Christ is the foundation of our nation, let us now look at the very first prayer offered in Congress on September 7, 1774 by Jacob Duche, "O Lord our Heavenly Father, high and mighty King of kings, and Lord of lords, who dost from thy throne behold all the dwellers on earth and reignest with power supreme and uncontrolled over all the Kingdoms, Empires, and Governments; look down in mercy, we beseech thee, on these our American States, who have fled to thee from the rod of the oppressor and thrown themselves on Thy gracious protection, desiring to be henceforth dependent only to Thee.... Give them wisdom in Council and valor in the field; defeat the malicious designs of our cruel adversaries;... constrain them to drop the weapons of war from their unnerved bands in the day of battle! Be Thou present, O God of wisdom, and direct the councils of this honorable assembly; enable them to settle things on the best and surest foundation. That the scene of blood may be speedily closed; that order, harmony, and peace may be effectually restored, and truth and justice, religion, and piety, prevail and flourish amongst the people.... All this we ask in the name and through the merits of Jesus Christ, Thy Son and our Savior. Amen."

President Thomas Jefferson made it clear, "The reason that Christianity is the best friend of government is because Christianity is the only religion that changes the heart."

American lexicographer Noah Webster (1758-1843) proclaimed, "The religion which has introduced civil liberty is the religion of Christ and His apostles... This is genuine Christianity, and to this we owe our free constitutions of government."

Yes, Jesus Christ changes hearts. The Bible describes Christ as the Word of God. Jesus was prophesied in the Old

Testament and was the fulfillment of prophecy in the New Testament. Whenever our national leaders referred to the Bible, they were referring to Christianity.

President Ronald Reagan declared 1983 as a National Year of the Bible. President Reagan explained, "Whereas, the Bible, the Word of God, has made a unique contribution in shaping the United States as a distinctive and blessed nation and people... Whereas that renewing our knowledge of and faith in God through Holy Scripture can strengthen us as a nation and a people: Now therefore, be it resolved... that the President is authorized and requested to designate 1983 as a National Year of the Bible."

Franklin Delano Roosevelt, our thirty-second President, said the following on an inscription in a special edition of the New Testament that was delivered to soldiers as they left for World War II, "As Commander-in-Chief, I take pleasure in commending the reading of the Bible to all who serve in the armed forces of the United States... It is a fountain of strength and now, as always, an aid in attaining the highest aspirations of the human soul."

Earlier, our twenty-eighth President, Woodrow Wilson explained, "When you have read the Bible, you will know it is the Word of God, because you will have found it the key to your own heart, your own happiness and your own duty."

President Wilson went on in 1913 to say, "I am sorry for the men who do not read the Bible every day. I wonder why they deprive themselves of the strength and of the pleasure."

And again President Wilson added, "The Bible... is the one supreme source of revelation of the meaning of life, the nature of God and the spiritual nature and needs of men. It is the only guide of life which really leads the spirit in the way of peace and salvation. **America was born a Christian nation. America was born to exemplify that devotion to the elements of righteousness which are derived from the revelations of Holy Scripture**."

As we see over and over again, Jesus Christ and the Bible are the heart and soul of America. The reason is simple: Jesus

Christ was and is the heart and soul to most of our Founding Fathers and even to many of our leaders today.

President Jimmy Carter made this comment during a 1976 interview, "We believe that the first time we're born, as children, it's human life given to us; and when we accept Jesus as our Savior, it's a new life. That's what 'born-again' means."

In 1954, President Dwight D. Eisenhower proclaimed, "The purpose of a devout and united people was set forth in the pages of the Bible... (1) to live in freedom (2) to work in a prosperous land... and (3) to obey the commandments of God... this biblical story of the promised land inspired the founders of America. It continues to inspire."

Once again we see the heart of American belief. In President John Quincy Adams' journal of 1814 he wrote, "My hopes of a future life are all founded upon the Gospel of Christ."

Again in the journal, President Adams wrote, "I speak as a man of the world to men of the world; and I say to you, Search the Scriptures! The Bible is the book of all others, to be read at all ages, and in all conditions..."

In 1831, John Quincy Adams made this bold declaration for the Word of God in a letter to His Son, "... So great is my veneration for the Bible, and so strong my belief, that when duly read and meditated on, it is of all books in the world, that which contributes most to make men good, wise and happy... I have myself, for many years, made it a practice to read through the Bible once every year."

President Theodore Roosevelt wrote, "The true Christian is the true citizen, lofty of purpose, resolute in endeavor, ready for a hero's deeds, but never looking down on his task because it is cast in the day of small things..."

In 1925, President Calvin Coolidge said during his Inaugural Address, "The higher state to which she (America) seeks the allegiance of all mankind is not human, but of Divine origin. She cherishes no purpose, save to merit the favor of Almighty God."

And later in his writings, President Coolidge confessed, "The foundations of our society and our governments rest so much on the teachings of the Bible that it would be difficult to support them if faith in these teachings would cease to be practically universal in our country."

Millions of Americans down through the ages have expressed a deep love and respect for Jesus Christ and the Bible. Our eighteenth President wrote the following letter in 1876 to the editor of the Sunday School Times in Philadelphia. President Ulysses S. Grant exhorted, "My advice to Sunday Schools, no matter what their denomination is: Hold fast to the Bible as the save anchor of your liberties; write its precepts in your hearts, and practice them in your lives. To the influence of this Book we are indebted for all the progress made in true civilization, and to this must we look as our guide in the future. 'Righteousness exalteth a nation; but sin is a reproach to any people.'"

And again President Grant wrote, "I believe in the Holy Scriptures, and whose lives by them will be benefited thereby. Men may differ as to the interpretation, which is human, but the Scriptures are man's best guide... I feel very grateful to the Christian people of the land for their prayers in my behalf. There is no sect or religion, as shown in the Old or New Testament, to which this does not apply."

In 1950, while addressing the United Nations, President Herbert Hoover wrote, "What the world needs today is a definite, spiritual mobilization of the nations who believe in God against this tide of Red agnosticism. It needs a moral mobilization against the hideous ideas of the police state and human slavery... I suggest that the United Nations should be reorganized without the Communist nations in it... And in rejecting an atheistic other world, I am confident that the Almighty God will be with us."

President Thomas Jefferson wrote in an 1803 letter to Dr. Benjamin Rush, "To the corruptions of Christianity I am, indeed, opposed; but not to the genuine precepts of Jesus himself. I am a Christian in the only sense in which he wished any one to be; sincerely attached to his doctrines in preference to all others."

Later, President Jefferson wrote, "A more beautiful or precious morsel of ethics I have never seen; it is a document in proof that I am a real Christian; that is to say, a disciple of the doctrines of Jesus."

And again President Jefferson reiterated, "Had the doctrines of Jesus been preached always as pure as they came from His lips, the whole civilized world would now have been Christians."

In his 1861 Inaugural Address, President Abraham Lincoln said, "Intelligence, patriotism, Christianity, and a firm reliance on Him who has never yet forsaken this favored land, are still competent to adjust in the best way all our present difficulty."

And later to his secretary, Noah Brooks, Abraham Lincoln confessed, "I have been driven many times upon my knees by the overwhelming conviction that I had nowhere else to go. My own wisdom, and that of all about me, seemed insufficient for that day."

Without a doubt, President Lincoln was a believer in Jesus Christ. Like most of our presidents and congressional leaders, he prayed, read his Bible and was a follower of Jesus Christ. In 1863, while proclaiming the first annual National Day of Thanksgiving, President Lincoln affirmed, "I do, therefore, invite my fellow citizens in every part of the United States, and those who are sojourning in foreign lands, to set apart and observe the last Thursday of November next as a day of Thanksgiving and Praise to our beneficent Father who dwelleth in the heavens... It has seemed to me fit and proper that God should be solemnly, reverently and gratefully acknowledged, as with one heart and one voice, by the whole American people."

Recently, while watching some classic Billy Graham Crusade videos, I came across the testimony of our forty-first President of the United States. President George Herbert Walker Bush stood tall in the pulpit and confessed his love and admiration for Jesus Christ.

In 1990, while declaring a National Day of Prayer, President Bush explained, "The great faith that led our nation's Founding Fathers to pursue this bold experience in self-government has sustained us in uncertain and perilous times; it has given us strength and inspiration to this very day. Like them, we do very well to recall our 'firm reliance on the protection of Divine Provident', to give thanks for the freedom and prosperity this nation enjoys, and to pray for continued help and guidance from our wise and loving Creator."

As a matter of fact, the past five Presidents of the United States all claimed to be followers of Jesus Christ. And not just in a religious sense, but in reality. These Presidents, some Republican and some Democrat, claimed to know Jesus Christ personally. They each acknowledged that Jesus Christ lived in their hearts.

Recently, I went fishing one night in the Gulf of Mexico. While I was baiting my hook, a total stranger came up and began to visit with me.

Within a few minutes, the subject changed to God, the Bible, and more specifically Jesus Christ. For the next two and a half hours, I witnessed to this man about the life and purpose of Jesus Christ. I also shared about the power of God to save, heal and to deliver. This man wanted to know all he could about Jesus Christ and the Holy Spirit.

Later that night, this fine southern gentleman prayed with me. He acknowledged his need for Christ and confessed his sins to God. He later shared how the meeting had changed his life. I came to find out that he was one of America's top attorneys and was just elected the Attorney General of one of America's great states.

During the course of our conversation, I discovered once again that Jesus Christ is the cry of the human heart. No matter how famous or rich you may be, your heart is empty until Jesus fills it with His love.

Yes, ladies and gentlemen, Jesus Christ is the heart and soul of America. He has blessed this country, and He is the God of our Founding Fathers, and He is the living Son of God.

True success depends on the "heart part." If you haven't given your heart to Christ, do it today. He will forgive you of all your sins, and He will give you everlasting life.

THREE

Jesus Is God

O ne of the great theologians of the twentieth century, C. S. Lewis once said, "As Christians we are tempted to make unnecessary concessions to those outside the Faith. We give in too much... there comes a time when we must show that we disagree. We must show our Christian colors if we are to be true to Christ. We cannot remain silent or concede anything away."

It's so easy to fall prey to political correctness and to become guilty of hiding your light. Mr. Lewis had it right, we should never concede anything away.

But all too often the Christian continues to sleep in harvest. We must wake out of sleep and put on the whole armor of God. It's time to take a stand for Jesus and to be a witness to a lost world.

Ravi Zacharas wrote in *Jesus Among Other Gods*, "We are living in a time when angry voices demand with increasing insistence that we ought not to propagate the gospel, that we ought not to consider anyone 'lost' just because they're not Christians. 'We are all born into different beliefs, and therefore, we should leave it that way,' so goes the tolerant 'wisdom' of our time... when people make such statements, they forget or do not know that one is not born a Christian. All Christians are such by virtue of conversion. To ask the Christian not to reach out to anyone else who is from another faith is to ask that Christian to deny his own faith."

The world's wisdom is foolishness with God. The apostle Paul wrote in 1 Corinthians 1:19-21:

For it is written, I will destroy the wisdom of the wise, and will bring to nothing the understanding of the prudent. Where is the wise? Where is the scribe? Where is the disputer of this world? Hath not God made foolish the wisdom of this world? For after that in the wisdom of God the world by wisdom knew not God, it pleased God by the foolishness of preaching to save them that believe.

Philosophy says, "Think your way out."
Industry says, "Work your way out."
Science says, "Invent your way out."
Religion says, "Earn your way out."
Fascism says, "Bluff your way out."
Militarism says, "Fight your way out."
Communism says, "Deceive your way out."
Education says, "Learn your way out."
But Jesus says, "**I am the way out.**"

John 14:6, "Jesus saith unto him, I am the Way, the Truth and the Life; no man cometh unto the Father but by me."

Friend, only Jesus forgives sin. You can take a sinner to college and he'll come out an educated sinner. You can take a sinner to church and he'll come out a religious sinner. You can take a sinner to the doctor and he'll come out a healthy sinner. You can take a sinner to a psychiatrist and he'll come out an adjusted sinner. But bring a sinner to Christ and he'll become a new creation.

For this reason and hundreds of others, we are compelled to speak the name of Jesus. In Philippians 2:6-11, we read:

Who, being in the form of God, thought it not robbery to be equal with God: but made Himself of no reputation, and took upon Him the form of a servant, and was made in the likeness of men: And being found in fashion as a man, He humbled Himself, and became obedient unto death, even the death of the cross. Wherefore God also hath highly exalted Him, and given Him a name which is above every name: That at the name of Jesus every knee should bow, of things in heaven, and things in earth, and things under the earth; and that every tongue should confess that Jesus Christ is Lord, to the glory of God the Father.

The Bible makes it clear that Jesus is the Son of God and that He is God the Son. However, many people do not understand the accomplishments of Christ nor his power. Likewise, even some Christians lack the basic knowledge of the deity of Christ.

The following Bible verses are just a few chosen versus that I picked out to prove the power, majesty, and deity of Jesus Christ. Hundreds of verses could be used, but for a lack of time and space, I have chosen just a few of the more obvious ones! You will discover, as have thousands of theologians, that Jesus Christ is coequal and co-eternal with God the Father.

John 1:1-5, " In the beginning was the Word and the Word was with God and the Word was God. The same was in the beginning with God. All things were made by Him and without Him was not anything made that was made. In Him was life; and the life was the light of men. And the light shineth in darkness and the darkness comprehended it not."

John 1:9, "That was the true light, which lighteth every man that cometh into the world."

John 1:10, "He was in the world and the world was made by Him and the world knew Him not."

John 1:12. "But as many as received Him, to them gave He power to become the sons of God, even to them that believe on His name."

John 1:13, "Which were born, not of blood, nor of the will of the flesh, nor of the will of man, but of God.

John 1:14, "And the Word was made flesh, and dwelt among us, (and we beheld His glory, the glory as of the only begotten of the Father), full of grace and truth."

These great Bible verses give us absolute clarity regarding the deity of Christ. Jesus was not a created being, but was the creator. It teaches that our Lord's personality and deity were without a beginning. Our Lord Jesus Christ did not become a person at his physical birth, nor did He somehow become God after His resurrection. Jesus is God from all of eternity.

Jesus Christ created all things visible and invisible (Colossians 1:16) including mankind, the animals, the heavenly planets, the angels etc...

Colossians 1:13-22 elaborates on this exciting subject:

Who hath delivered us from the power of darkness, and hath translated us into the kingdom of His dear Son: In whom we have redemption through His blood, even the forgiveness of sins: Who is the image of the invisible God, the firstborn of every creature: For by Him were all things created. That are in heaven, and that are in earth, visible and invisible, whether they be thrones, or dominions, or principalities, or powers: all things were created by Him, and for Him: And He is before all things, and by Him all things consist. And He is the head of the body, the church: who is the beginning, the firstborn from the dead; that in all things He might have the preeminence. For it pleased the Father that in Him should all fullness dwell; And, having made peace through the blood of His cross, by Him to reconcile all things unto Himself; by Him, I say, whether they be things in earth, or things in heaven. And you, that were sometime alienated and enemies in your mind by wicked works, yet now hath He reconciled in the body of His flesh through death, to present you holy and unblameable and unreproveable in His sight.

Without a doubt, Jesus Christ is the architect of the universe. He created everything visible and invisible (angels, thrones, principalities, dominions and powers). Jesus is before all things and in Christ do all things consist.

Jesus Christ is the sustainer of the universe and the source of its perpetual motion. He controls the stars, and the sun, and the moon.

The dominion of the Lord Jesus not only extends to the natural universe, but also covers the spiritual realm. Jesus is also the head of the body, the church. The head speaks of authority, guidance, dictation, and control. He occupies the place of preeminence in the church, but also preeminence in creation. God has decreed that in all things, Christ must have the preeminence. Alfred Mace put it well, "Thus creation and redemption hand the honors of supremacy to Him because of who He is and of what He has done ' that in all things He might have the preeminence'. He is first everywhere."

According to the proper translation of verse 19, Darby says, "For in Him all the fullness of the Godhead was pleased to dwell." This literally means that the fullness of the Godhead always dwelt in Christ.

In verse 20, we discover that it pleased the Father not only that all fullness should dwell in Christ, but also that Christ should reconcile all things to Himself. This reconciliation means literally both all things and the reconciliation of persons. All things include all future events and reconciliation of mankind is the redemption found only in Christ.

In 2 Corinthians 5:18-21, we read a further explanation regarding our Lord's ministry of reconciliation:

> And all things are of God, who hath reconciled us to Himself by Jesus Christ, and hath given to us the ministry of reconciliation; to wit, that God was in Christ, reconciling the world unto Himself, not imputing their trespasses unto them; and hath committed unto us the Word of reconciliation. Now then we are ambassadors for Christ, as though God did beseech you by us: we pray you in Christ's stead, be ye reconciled to God. For He hath made Him to be sin for us, who knew no sin; that we might be made the righteousness of God in Him.

Ladies and gentlemen, simply put, Jesus Christ is Lord. He is God the Son and the Son of God for all of eternity.

First Timothy 3:16 reads, "And without controversy, great is the mystery of godliness. God was manifested in the flesh, justified in the spirit, seen of angels, preached unto the Gentiles, believed on in the world, received up into glory."

In John 8:58, Jesus explains who He is, "Jesus said unto them, 'Verily, verily, I say unto you, Before Abraham was, I am.'"

This so infuriated the Jews that they took up rocks to stone Christ. Why? Because Jesus was saying "I am God." Christ was saying the same thing the Father God Jehovah said in Exodus 3:14, "I AM THAT I AM."

The prophet Isaiah looked into the future and under the prophetic anointing of the Holy Spirit he wrote, "For unto us a child is born, unto us the Son is given; and the Government shall be upon His shoulder and His name shall be called Wonderful, Counselor, the Mighty God, the Everlasting Father, the Prince of Peace" (Isaiah 9:6).

In Matthew 1:18-24, we read of the supernatural birth of our Lord Jesus Christ. In these verses we see God the Father, God the Son, and God the Holy Spirit all actively working together as one God:

> Now the birth of Jesus Christ was on this wise: when as His mother Mary was espoused to Joseph, before they came together, she was found with child of the Holy Ghost. Then Joseph her husband, being a just man, and not willing to make her a public example, was minded to put her away privily. But while he thought on these things, behold, the angel of the Lord appeared unto him in a dream, saying, Joseph, thou son of David, fear not to take unto thee Mary thy wife: for that which is conceived in her is of the Holy Ghost. And she shall bring forth a Son, and thou shalt call his name JESUS: for He shall save his people from their sins. Now all this was done, that it might be fulfilled which was spoken of the Lord by the prophet, saying, Behold, a virgin shall be with child, and shall bring forth a Son, and they shall call His name Emmanuel, which being interpreted is, God with us. Then Joseph being raised from sleep did as the angel of the Lord had bidden him, and took unto him his wife:

and knew her not till she had brought forth her firstborn Son: and he called His name JESUS.

Yes, ladies and gentlemen, Jesus Christ is Lord to the glory of the Father. Jesus is God the Son and the Son of God. He is coequal and co-eternal with the Father and with the Holy Ghost. In a later chapter, we will discuss the Trinity in more detail.

When we read that Christ Jesus was in the form of God, we learn that He existed from all of eternity. It does not mean that He merely resembled God, but that He actually is God in the truest sense of the word.

Ephesians 1:17-23 proclaims:

> That the God of our Lord Jesus Christ, the Father of glory, may give unto you the spirit of wisdom and revelation in the knowledge of Him: the eyes of your understanding being enlightened; that ye may know what is the hope of His calling, and what the riches of the glory of His inheritance in the saints, and what is the exceeding greatness of His power to us-ward who believe, according to the working of His mighty power, which He wrought in Christ, when He raised Him from the dead, and set Him at His own right hand in the heavenly places, far above all principality, and power, and might, and dominion, and every name that is named, not only in this world, but also in that which is to come: and hath put all things under His feet, and gave Him to be the head over all things to the church, which is His body, the fullness of Him that filleth all in all.

In Colossians 2:6-15, we read a further description regarding the power of the Gospel of Jesus Christ:

> As ye have therefore received Christ Jesus the Lord, so walk ye in Him: rooted and built up in Him, and stablished in the faith, as ye have been taught, abounding therein with thanksgiving. Beware lest any man spoil you

through philosophy and vain deceit after the tradition of men, after the rudiments of the world, and not after Christ. For in Him dwelleth all the fullness of the Godhead bodily. And ye are complete in Him, which is the head of all principality and power: In whom also ye are circumcised with the circumcision made without hands, in putting off the body of the sins of the flesh by the circumcision of Christ: Buried with Him in Baptism, wherein also ye are risen with Him through the faith of the operation of God, who hath raised Him from the dead. And you, being dead in your sins and the uncircumcision of your flesh, hath He quickened together with Him, having forgiven you all trespasses; Blotting out the handwriting of ordinances that was against us, which was contrary to us, and took it out of the way, nailing it to His cross; And having spoiled principalities and powers, He made a shew of them openly, triumphing over them in it.

In 1 John 5:4-13, we read a beautiful depiction of the entire salvation plan that includes the work of God the Father, God the Son, and God the Holy Spirit:

For whatsoever is born of God overcometh the world: and this is the victory that overcometh the world, even our faith. Who is He that overcometh the world, but he that believeth that Jesus is the Son of God? This is He that came by water and blood, even Jesus Christ; not by water only, but by water and blood. And it is the Spirit that beareth witness, because the Spirit is truth. For there are three that bear record in heaven, the Father, the Word, and the Holy Ghost: and these three are one. And they are three that bear witness in Earth, the Spirit, and the Water, and the Blood: and these three agree in one. If we receive the witness of men, the witness of God is greater: for this is the witness of God which he hath testified of His Son. He that believeth on the Son of God hath the witness in himself: he that believeth not God hath made him a liar; because he believeth not the record that God gave his son. And this is the record, that

God hath given to us eternal life, and this life is in His Son. He that hath the Son hath life; and he that hath not the Son of God hath not life. These things have I written unto you that believe on the name of the Son of God; that ye may know that ye have eternal life, and that ye may believe on the name of the Son of God.

In 1 John 5:19-20: "And we know that we are of God, and the whole world lieth in wickedness. And we know that the Son of God is come, and hath given us an understanding, that we may know Him that is true, and we are in Him that is true, even in his Son Jesus Christ. This is the true God, and eternal life."

Even though I could write a ten thousand page book on the deity of Christ, I must, at least offer a few key verses. Later in this book you will see many other examples of the deity of Christ. In Hebrews 1:1-10, it says:

God, who at sundry times and in divers manners spake in time past unto fathers by the prophets, hath in these last days spoken unto us by His Son, whom He hath appointed heir of all things, by whom also He made the worlds; Who being the brightness of His glory, and the express image of His person, and upholding all things by the Word of His power, when He had by Himself purged our sins, sat down on the right hand of the Majesty on high; Being made so much better than the angels, as He hath by inheritance obtained a more excellent name than they. For unto which of the angels said He at any time, Thou art my Son, this day have I begotten thee? And again, I will be to Him a Father, and He shall be to me a Son? And again, when He bringeth in the first begotten into the world, he saith, And let all the angels of God worship Him. And of the angels He saith, Who maketh His angels spirits, and His ministers a flame of fire. But unto the Son He saith, Thy throne, O God, is for ever and ever: a sceptre of righteousness is the sceptre of thy kingdom. Thou hast loved righteousness, and hated iniquity; therefore God, even thy God, hath anointed thee with oil of gladness above thy fellows. And, Thou, Lord, in the beginning hast laid the foundation of the earth; and the heavens are the works of thine hands.

In Hebrews 2:8-10:

Thou hast put all things in subjection under His feet. For in that He put all in subjection under Him, He left nothing that is not put under Him. But now we see not yet all things put under Him. But we see Jesus, who was made a little lower than the angels for the suffering of death, crowned with glory and honor; that He by the grace of God should taste death for every man. For it became Him, for whom are all things, and by whom are all things, in bringing many sons unto glory, to make the captain of their salvation perfect through sufferings.

Once again let me emphasize the importance of speaking the name of Jesus. His name must be glorified in you. In 2 Thessalonians 1:12, it reads, "That the name of our Lord Jesus Christ may be glorified in you, and ye in Him, according to the grace of our God and the Lord Jesus Christ."

Our founding fathers based this nation on the name that is above every name. They continually honored the name of Jesus Christ from the beginning of this country right up to 1963. After that year, demonic forces in this country have used various liberal groups to try to push His name out of our culture.

The whole idea of the separation of church and state is a misnomer. It's simply **NOT** in the constitution. The first amendment actually reads, "Congress shall make no law respecting an establishing of religion or prohibiting the free exercise thereof."

The early Supreme Court and Congress properly interpreted this to mean the government cannot choose one Christian religion over another. In other words, they didn't want America to be like England in that the government becomes an official religion. And in the eyes of our founding fathers the only religion that defined America was the Christian religion. When they spoke of God, they spoke only of the God of Christianity.

In 1796, the Supreme Court made a ruling on Runkel vs. Winemiller. Their conclusion, decision and judgment read, "By our form of government, the Christian religion and all sects and denominations of Christians are placed on the same equal footing."

Later in 1892, the Supreme Court ruled on the Church of the Holy Trinity vs. U.S. In it, our Supreme Court concluded, "Our laws and our institutions must necessarily be based upon and embody the teachings of the Redeemer of mankind, and it's impossible that it should be otherwise; and in this sense and to this extent our civilization and our institutions are emphatically Christian."

The early leaders of our country and right up to the twentieth century were 100 percent sold on the fact that for America to prosper she must serve Jesus Christ and obey the Bible. They believed with their whole hearts that Jesus Christ was GOD and deserved to be worshiped as the Redeemer of mankind.

When Benjamin Franklin was our American ambassador to France, he wrote, "Whoever will introduce into public affairs the Principles of Christianity will change the face of the world."

Our educational system was likewise built on the foundation of the Bible and faith in Jesus Christ. For some two hundred years, the alphabet was taught using various Bible verses. Furthermore, class Bible reading and praying were the norm for everyday school life.

A nation without Jesus is a nation without God. Jesus said in Matthew 10:32-33, "Whosoever therefore shall confess me before men, him will I confess also before my Father which is in Heaven. But whosoever shall deny me before men, him will I also deny before my Father which is in Heaven."

In John 14:1-3, Jesus promised, "Let not your heart be troubled, ye believe in God, believe also in me. In my Father's house are many mansions, if it were not so, I would of told you, I go to prepare a place for you. And if I go to prepare a place for you, I will come again and receive you unto myself, that where I am, there you may be also."

Then Jesus went on and said in John 14:13-14, "And whatsoever ye shall ask in my name, that will I do, that the Father may be glorified in the Son. If ye shall ask anything in my name, I will do it."

Now the name of Jesus is the most powerful name on earth. But in the Word of God, we discover Jesus is given other names that likewise show forth His power. In Matthew 1:23 it promises, "Behold a virgin shall be with child and shall bring forth a Son and they shall call His name Emmanuel, which being interpreted is, God with us."

Besides the name Emmanuel, Jesus is also referred to in Scripture as:

Savior, The Christ, The Son of God, Lord of All, Our Savior Jesus Christ, King of Kings, The Word, Wonderful, Counselor, Alpha and Omega, The Lord, The Beginning and the End, Lord of Lords, The Way, The Truth, The Life, The Almighty, The Prince of Peace, First and Last, God Blessed Forever, The Father of Eternity, The Holy One, Jehovah, The Mighty God, My Lord and My God, and The Great God.

Jesus Himself was a fulfillment of Bible prophesies. Christ fulfilled 109 prophecies that were predicted five hundred to fifteen hundred years before His birth.

Jesus Christ literally changed the world. Our historical calendar is based on His existence. Every year we celebrate Christmas (His Birthday), Good Friday (His Crucifixion) and Easter (His Resurrection). Because of Jesus Christ, women and children have been given dignity. The marriage of a man and a woman was sanctioned by Jesus Christ and has been the moral rock of every civilized people. Because of Jesus, our world has been taught morals; to know good from evil. Jesus taught us to love our neighbor and to pray for them that despitefully use us.

Thousands of hospitals, orphan homes, relief centers and shelters have helped millions of lives because of Jesus Christ. America and the free world can trace their freedoms to the teachings of the Son of God. Christ has given us the greatest music, art, and devotion that man has ever seen. His influence has changed the course of education and governments for centuries. The good we experience is because of Jesus Christ. The bad we encounter is because of Biblical disobedience. He is Light and in Jesus is no darkness at all.

Jesus is the only one who did anything for sinners. Only by His blood can a man or a woman be washed clean from his or her sins and inherit everlasting life. In John 15:13, Jesus said, "Greater love hath no man than this, that a man lay down his life for his friends."

Jesus Christ promised us Peace, because He is the Prince of Peace. He promised us Love because Christ is Love. He promised Joy because He is Joy. He promised everlasting life because He is the resurrection and the life.

That's why the early disciples confessed in Acts, "In Him we move, live and have our being" (Acts 17:28).

Jesus said in John 16:33, "These things I have spoken unto you, that in me ye might have peace. In the world ye shall have tribulations; but be of good cheer; I have overcome the world."

The apostle John summed up the life and works of Jesus Christ when he wrote, "And there are also many other things which Jesus did, the which, if they should be written every one, I suppose that even the world itself could not contain the books that should be written. Amen" (John 21:25).

Ladies and gentlemen, simply put, Jesus Christ is God. He is the God our founding fathers worshiped and adored. He is the God of America. To deny Christ is to deny ourselves. That's why America needs to say Jesus!

One anointed writer described the life and impact of Christ in this writing called "One Solitary Life":

He was born in an obscure village, the child of a peasant woman. He grew up in another obscure village, where He worked in a carpenter shop until He was thirty.

Then for three years He was an itinerant preacher. He never had a family or owned a home. He never set foot inside a big city. He never traveled two hundred miles from the place He was born. He never wrote a book or held an office. He did none of the things that usually accompany greatness.

While He was still a young man, the tide of popular opinion turned against Him. His friends deserted Him. He was turned over to His enemies and went through the mockery of a trial. He was nailed to a cross between two thieves. While He was dying, His executioners gambled for the only piece of property He had—His coat. When He was dead, He was taken down and laid in a borrowed grave.

Nineteen centuries have come and gone, and today He is the central figure for much of the human race. All the armies that ever marched, and all the navies that ever sailed, and all the parliaments that ever sat, and all the kings that ever reigned, put together, have not affected the life of man upon this earth as powerfully as this one solitary life.

Mark 16:19-20, "So then after the Lord had spoken unto them, He was received up into heaven, and sat on the right hand of God. And they went forth, and preached every where, the Lord working with them, and confirming the word with signs following. Amen."

John 14:27, Jesus promised, "Peace, I leave with you, my peace I give unto you: not as the world giveth, give I unto you. Let not your heart be troubled, neither let it be afraid."

John 15:11, Jesus continued, "These things have I spoken unto you, that my joy might remain in you and that your joy might be full."

And now one of the greatest attorneys of all time, Dr. Sir Lionel Luckhoo, sums up his proof of the Resurrection of Jesus Christ, His deity, and the accuracy of the Word of God. Dr. Luckhoo writes:

"In summary form we can say:

- The Bible proves itself;
- It is God-breathed, showing an amazing unity of the forty diverse authors;

- It is indestructible, despite all the persecutions;
- Its historical accuracy was confirmed time and time again;
- Its scientific accuracy has time and again been proven even to the discovery of the day the sun stood still; (Joshua 10:13), *'And the sun stood still, and the moon stayed, until the people had avenged themselves upon their enemies.'* And that the earth was round (Isaiah 40:22), *'It is he that sitteth upon the circle of the earth...'*

"Finally, hundreds of prophecies have been foretold and have all come to pass, strictly as predicted.

"We now await, I repeat, the fulfillment of the prophecy that could come to pass at any time now, and that is the return of Jesus when the dead in Christ and the living believers will be caught up in the Rapture to be with him for always, in the place he has prepared for them."

Sir Lionel Luckhoo in his book, *What Is Your Verdict?* writes the following about Jesus Christ: "Jesus was born about 4 B.C. in Bethlehem of Judea. In the one person there were two natures, a human nature and a divine nature, each in its completeness and integrity, yet as A.H. Strong puts it, 'These two natures were organically and indissoluble united, so that no third nature is formed thereby.'

"He was born of Mary, and so was wholly man. He had no human father; He was born by the will of God and so was wholly God. His birth was natural; it was his conception that was supernatural. In like form, his death was natural but his resurrection was supernatural.

"His birth was foretold many times in the Bible. Here are just three examples, Isaiah 7:14, written 750 years before Jesus' birth, *'Therefore the Lord himself shall give you a sign; Behold a virgin shall conceive, and bear a son, and shall call his name Immanuel.'*

"Isaiah 9:6, *'For unto us as child is born, unto us a Son is given: and the government shall be upon His shoulder: and His name shall be called Wonderful, Counsellor, The mighty God, The everlasting Father, the Prince of Peace.'*

"Then in Micah 5:2, *'But thou, Bethlehem Ephratah, though thou be little among the thousands of Judah, yet out of thee shall he come forth unto me that is to be ruler in Israel; whose goings forth have been from of old, from everlasting.'*

"For a prophecy to be accepted, it must be shown it was made before, it was fulfilled later, and fulfilled in ever-material particular. The Dead Sea Scrolls containing the whole of Isaiah found in 1947 verify that Isaiah was written centuries before the birth of Jesus. This was verified by paleographers and after carbon 14 tests were taken. So the prophecies were made before the birth of Jesus and fulfilled subsequently."

Why Jesus Came

"Why did Jesus come to earth? Jesus was preexistent. He was with God before time began. He came as the Son of God to shed His blood, to give His life voluntarily for us, because the first Adam committed treason and sinned and so brought death to the world. Adam did this voluntarily, so Jesus had to voluntarily give His life that we could once again inherit eternal life, but Jesus did more than that. He took our sins upon Himself so that we are washed clean, and as we invite Jesus to come into our hearts, to be our Lord and Master, we are regenerated. We move from death to life; from darkness to light we are born again.

"How does this all fit in with the salvation pattern? It does so four square. But since the Mormons, Jehovah's Witnesses, and several other alleged Christian groups deny the deity of Jesus, let me carry out a brief exercise to allay their doubt, and maybe yours too, members of the jury."

Deity of Jesus by Accreditation

"The Deity of Jesus is revealed to us by his accreditation to the people of the world by the Father, as Peter in Acts 2:22 puts it; *'Ye men of Israel, hear these words; Jesus of Nazareth, a man approved of God among you by miracles and wonders and signs, which God did by him in the midst of you, as ye yourselves also know:'*

Peter was referring to:

- His virgin birth;

- That no one before or since ever spoke with such learning and knowledge;
- His miracles they all saw; He revived the dead, healed the sick, made the dumb speak, etc.; He controlled nature, the waves, the sea, the wind; He produced bread and fish, produced literally from nothing, to feed multi-thousands;
- Then Jesus conquered the grave; to die no more;
- Every promise Jesus made He kept and He has promised us life eternal or everlasting life. He has promised us salvation.

"I would like to put some of these a little differently. In the courts we sometimes call a person to testify as an expert witness. He is subjected to the most careful, intensive cross-examination before the court will rule on whether he is an expert. If he is not, his expert evidence is shut out. If the court rules in his favor, his evidence is accepted."

Expert Witness

"Well, let us look at Jesus in this light. Is he an expert witness qualified to testify as to what lies beyond the portals of death? Indeed, He is the only one so qualified to speak. The actuality of Christ's resurrection is a proper subject for the most careful scrutiny. His testimony is unshakable. Add to this the supportive evidence of the empty tomb. His eleven appearances and on one occasion before more than five hundred, this is so powerful that His evidence must be accepted and He must be deemed the only expert witness on this aspect. It should not be overlooked that the Gospel has as its factual foundation, events that happened at the world's most cultured, cynical and skeptical age. That this all happened at that time lends credence to all that took place.

"Ladies and Gentlemen of the jury, do you think the eyewitnesses who testified were lying? If so, for what reward? For torture and for death? He spoke to them. He ate with them. Clearly they were telling the truth about an unmistakable fact that manifested to them as to make the whole Roman Empire unable to shake their testimony or stem the tide of their evangelism.

"Because of what took place, the most ancient of all memorial institutions, the Sabbath Day, was abandoned, and another day observed from the Resurrection of Christ to commemorate that event until now."

Evidence of Jesus' Deity

"If I may be pardoned the liberty, in a court of law to establish the Deity of Jesus, I would call with all respect and deference my Lord Jesus on to the witness stand and ask him: Lord Jesus, whom did you say you are? Jesus' replies are found in the Bible:

- *'I am the Resurrection and the Life; if a man believes in me, though he were dead yet shall he live, and he that liveth and believeth in me shall never die.'* (John 11:25)
- *'Before Abraham was born I am.'* (John 8:58)
- *'I and the Father are one.'* (John 10:30)
- *'Ye believe in God also believe in me.'* (John 14:1)
- *'I am the Christ.'* (Mark 14:62)

"Let us also examine in brief what Almighty God said about Jesus: At the baptism and transfiguration of Jesus, God spoke and said, *'This is my Son whom I love, with Him I am well pleased.'* (Matthew 3:17 and Matthew 17:5) and again in Psalms 2:7, *'You are my Son. Today I have become your Father.'*

"What did the angel Gabriel say about Jesus? *'Fear not, I bring you good tidings of great joy... unto you is born this day in the City of David a Saviour which is Christ the Lord.'* (Luke 4:10) We all know that Peter proclaimed Jesus as *'The Christ, the Son of the Living God.'* (Matthew 16:16) But in this trial within a trial, I would like to call and confound Satan with his admissions. There is no stronger evidence then citing that your opponents aver, and in this instance I say to Satan and his demons, whom do you say is this Jesus?

"The answers are given in Mark 1:24, Mark 3:11, Mark 5:7 and Luke 4:33:

Mark 1:24, *'What do you want with us, Jesus of Nazareth? Have you come to destroy us? I know who You are- The Holy One of God.'*

Mark 3:11, *'Whenever the evil spirits saw Him, they fell down before Him and cried out, You are the Son of God.'*

Mark 5:7, *'... What have I to do with thee, Jesus, thou Son of the most high God?'*

"What greater proof as to the deity, that Jesus is the Holy Son of God, than the very words out of the mouth of Satan and his demon colleagues?

"Finally I would call onto the witness stand the Centurion, who with his soldiers took Jesus to Calvary and crucified him. What, sir, do you have to say about Jesus? His reply comes from the Bible, Matthew 27:54: When the earth did quake and veils rent, the centurion said, *'Truly this was the Son of God.'* Yes, from the lips of his executioner comes this declaration. How then, alleged Christians and supposed Believers, can you ever doubt the Deity of Jesus?

"At this stage of our arguments we have put forward for your conversation and acceptance:

- That there is a God, a power infinite which our finite minds cannot fully or even partially comprehend;
- That to give to you and to me and to all mankind eternal life, God sent His only son Jesus to die on the cross for our redemption and to wipe the slate clean of the inglorious treason of Adam;
- Because God gave Adam and all mankind free choice, Adam voluntarily committed sin and brought death to the world, so God gave us His son Jesus and we are required voluntarily to accept Him, to invite Him into our hearts.
- Now you too, members of the jury, can regain the life eternal but you must voluntarily accept and ask Jesus to come into your heart and so be born-again;
- All of these aspects are fully dealt with in the Christian Bible which I pointed out ought to be accepted by everyone. But let us continue."

Secular Historians

"Ladies and gentlemen of the jury, although I feel we have established our case literally to the hilt, let me quote from the secular historians of the period during which Jesus lived. Foremost among them was the non-Christian Flavius Josephus. Josephus was of a Jewish family, well-educated, of the pharisaic form of Judaism. In AD 66-70, he commanded the Jewish force in Galilee; he went to Rome with Titus, helping the Romans by making the Jews come to terms. He was a close friend of the Emperors Vespasian and Titus, and took their family name Flavius. He was the most distinguished and noteworthy historian of the early period during which Jesus lived.

"Josephus wrote in his *Antiquities of the Jews* Book VIII, Chapter II: 'Now there was about this time Jesus, a wise man, for He was the doer of wonderful works, a teacher, of such men as receive the truth with pleasure. He drew over to Him, both many of the Jews and many of the Gentiles. He was the Christ; and when Pilate at the suggestion of the principal amongst us had condemned Him to the cross, those that loved Him and did not forsake Him, for He appeared to them alive again the third day as the divine prophets had foretold; these and ten thousand other wonderful things concerning Him and the tribe of Christians so named from Him are not extinct at this day.'

"This citation was accepted, relied upon and repeated by all the subsequent historians. It must be treated as if I was quoting Arnold Toynbee. A historian records facts, not his own views. Josephus lived and wrote at a time when eyewitnesses were alive, who saw Jesus crucified, saw His empty tomb, saw Him come back to preach and teach. This gave Peter the courage to proclaim Jesus in Jerusalem, the very place where He was crucified and where He appeared again. Eusebius, Tacitus, and all subsequent historians refer to the authority of Flavius Josephus.

"Paul puts it with logic and reason in Romans 6:9, *'For we know that since Christ was raised from the dead, He cannot die again; death no longer has mastery over Him, the death He died to sin once and for all, but the life He lives He lives to God.'* "

Ladies and gentlemen, there is absolutely no doubt that Jesus Christ is God. He is one with the Father and the Holy Spirit. He lived a sinless life, died for our sins and rose again triumphant. This same Jesus turned water into wine, walked on the water, stopped a raging storm, healed all manner of sickness and even raised the dead. Christ gave sight to the blind and hope to the hopeless and He cast out devils. Christ took five loaves of bread and two small fish and fed five thousand men. Jesus himself confessed to be God. He said:

- "I am the good Shepherd, the good shepherd giveth His life for the sheep" (John 10:11).
- "I am the vine, ye are the branches. He that abideth in me and I in him, the same bringeth forth much fruit; for without me ye can do nothing" (John 15:5).
- "I am the Resurrection and the life: he that believeth in me though he were dead, yet shall he live" (John 11:25).
- "I am the door; by me if any man enter in, he shall be saved, and shall go in and out, and find pasture" (John 10:9).
- "I am the light of the world: he that followeth me shall not walk in darkness, but shall have the light of life" (John 8:12).
- "I am the bread of life: he that cometh to me shall never hunger; and he that believeth on me shall never thirst" (John 6:35).
- Jesus said unto them, verily, verily, I say unto you, Before Abraham I am. (John 8:58).

FOUR

Power in the Name of Jesus

My father was dying with an incurable disease. He was given only a few months to live. However, a pastor prayed in Jesus' name, and my dad was totally healed by the power of God.

Doctors told my wife that she wouldn't be able to have children, but a man of God prayed in Jesus' name, and today we have three beautiful children.

While preaching in Ethiopia, I prayed in Jesus' name, and hundreds of sick people were instantly healed. Four men in comas awoke giving glory to God. A girl, who was paralyzed from the waist down, got off her stretcher and walked.

In Kerala, India over ten thousand demon-possessed Hindus were delivered in one service. Demons came screaming out when I prayed in the name of Jesus.

In hundreds of the churches I have ministered in, I can witness to the fact that thousands of people were instantly delivered from drugs and alcohol by the name of Jesus.

Millions upon millions of people have testified throughout the world that the name of Jesus has changed their lives. Throughout the ages, Jesus Christ has healed people physically, emotionally, and spiritually. And He hasn't changed. The Bible declares that Jesus Christ is the same yesterday, today, and forever.

The motivation of Mel Gibson's movie *The Passion of the Christ* was from Mr. Gibson's own experience with Jesus. He said, "His stripes healed my wounds."

Every time the name of Jesus is spoken by faith, something supernatural takes place. For this reason, Satan has done everything conceivable to stop the name of Jesus. In many Islamic countries, it is illegal to even witness in Jesus' name to a Muslim. And here in America, lawsuits are continually being filed to keep people from saying "Jesus."

This conspiracy to stop the name of Jesus actually began in the book of Acts! The disciples were warned in Acts 5:28, "Did we not straitly command you that ye should not teach in this name? And behold ye have filled Jerusalem with your doctrine and ye intend to bring this man's blood upon us."

It was made very clear to the disciples—don't preach or teach in the name of Jesus. But that wasn't all, for in Acts 5:40 the warning goes one step further. Acts 5:40 reads, "and when they had called the apostles and beaten them, they commanded that they should not speak in the name of Jesus and let them go."

In other words, don't teach in His name, don't preach in His name, and don't even *speak* in the name of Jesus.

The answer of the disciples should also be our answer today. Their witness continued, "And daily in the Temple and in every house, they ceased not to teach and preach Jesus Christ" (Acts 5:42).

And Peter's response to an earlier threat was this, "We ought to obey God rather than men" (Acts 5:29).

When further threatened, the apostle Peter prayed, "And now, Lord behold their threatenings and grant unto thy servants that with all boldness they may speak thy Word. By stretching forth thine hand to heal; and that signs and wonders may be done by the name of the holy child Jesus" (Acts 4:29-30).

You must understand what the early church knew and what the unsaved religious leaders feared. There's power in the name of Jesus. The religious leaders saw their place of prominence slipping because of Jesus Christ. At one point—**before Christ's crucifixion and resurrection**—they said, "If we don't kill Jesus, all men will believe in Him."

Now as the new church of Christ was emerging faster and faster, they discovered the source of the growth was the name of Jesus Christ. When Christians spoke the name of Jesus, souls were saved, lives changed, and bodies healed. Every time the disciples preached in the name of Jesus, miracles occurred and the people left their dead religions and converted to Christianity. The only way the religious leaders and the demons of hell could stop the growth of Christianity was by forbidding the use of Jesus. And so it is today. Throughout the world, there is a demonic conspiracy to stop the name of Jesus from flowing out of the mouths of Christ's followers. In the minds of secular humanists, the only time Christ or the name of Jesus should be used is in swearing.

The anti-Christ crowd two thousand years ago is demonically linked and related to the same anti-Christ crowd of today. They hate the name of Jesus, because it makes their dead philosophers and religions void. The name of Jesus exposes their sin, their hypocrisy and their demonic activity. They know that when Jesus is freely spoken and proclaimed entire cities have been known to convert to Christianity.

The Muslims fear the name of Jesus. In most Muslim countries, you can be jailed, even killed, for using Christ's name to convert others. Likewise, Hindus, Buddhists, and most religions and occults have come against the name of Jesus. Their false gods are exposed by the name of Jesus. The ACLU and their cronies despise the freedom Americans have to speak Jesus. That's why so many lawsuits are being filed against Christian prayers, crosses, nativity scenes, etc... Likewise, Hollywood hates the name of Jesus. His name and His Word expose their filth and their new age, but old immorality.

You see friend, God the Father chose God the Son to be the Redeemer of mankind. God the Father chose God the Holy Spirit to reveal Jesus to the whole world. It's only through Christ that a person can get to heaven. Jesus said in John 3:3, "Verily, verily, I say unto thee, Except a man be born again, he cannot see the kingdom of God."

The Bible makes it clear that only in Christ can you become a new creation. Only by Christ's blood can your sins be washed clean. And it's only by the power of the Holy Spirit that you can be a witness for Christ.

God the Father also made it clear that the final judgment of mankind is given to Jesus Christ.

For this reason and hundreds of others, Satan hates Jesus Christ and despises His name. And the unsaved and ungodly hate Christ because Jesus is the Light. His light exposes the darkness of their lives. Therefore, we see this cultural war being played out everyday in our schools, businesses, and in our government. They want to stop the name of Jesus, and we want to proclaim the name of Jesus. That is the battlefield!

Jesus said in Mark 16:17-18, "And these signs shall follow them that believe; In my name shall they cast out devils; they shall speak with new tongues; They shall take up serpents; and if they drink any deadly thing, it shall not hurt them; they shall lay hands on the sick, and they shall recover."

Yes friend, there is power in the name of Jesus. In Acts 3:6-20, we read the amazing healing of a crippled man who was begging by the gate of the temple, which was called Beautiful. These verses not only describe the healing, they also explain that the healing occurred due to the faith that was in the name of Jesus. Furthermore, the writer of Acts tells men and women everywhere what they must do as individuals to have peace with God.

> Then Peter said, Silver and gold have I none; but such as I have give I thee: In the name of Jesus Christ of Nazareth rise up and walk. And he took him by the right hand, and lifted him up: and immediately his feet and ankle bones received strength. And he leaping up stood, and walked, and entered with them into the temple, walking and leaping, and praising God. And all the people saw him walking and praising God: And they knew that it was he which sat for alms at the Beautiful gate of the temple: and they were filled with wonder and amazement at that which had happened unto him. And as the lame man which was healed held Peter and John, all the people ran together unto them in the porch that is called Solomon's, greatly wondering. And when Peter saw it, he answered unto the people, Ye men of Israel, why marvel ye at this?

Or why look ye so earnestly on us, as though by our own power or holiness we had made this man to walk? The God of Abraham, and of Isaac, and of Jacob, the God of our fathers, hath glorified his Son Jesus; whom ye delivered up, and denied Him in the presence of Pilate, when he was determined to let Him go. But ye denied the Holy One and the Just, and desired a murderer to be granted unto you; And killed the Prince of life, whom God hath raised from the dead; whereof we are witnesses. And His name through faith in His name hath made this man strong, whom ye see and know: yea, the faith which is by Him hath given this perfect soundness in the presence of you all. And now brethren, I wot that through ignorance ye did it, as did also your rulers. But those things, which God before has shewed by the mouth of all his prophets, that Christ should suffer, He hath so fulfilled. Repent ye therefore, and be converted, that your sins may be blotted out, when the times of refreshing shall come from the presence of the Lord; And He shall send Jesus Christ, which before was preached unto you.

Yes, there is power in the name of Jesus. Demons tremble at just the sound of that name, Jesus! The anti-Christ movement hates the name of Jesus. His name represents light, freedom, and stands for righteousness. Their lives are filled with darkness, bondage, and they stand for wickedness. As a result, they are pawns in Satan's hands to fight Christianity. However, no matter how hard they may try, the name of Jesus can never be replaced or destroyed. His name is above **EVERY** name!

In the book of Philippians 2:10-11 it reads, "That at the name of Jesus every knee should bow of things in heaven and things in earth and things under the earth. And that every tongue should confess that Jesus Christ is Lord, to the glory of God the Father."

And again the apostle Peter reiterates on the healing power in Jesus' name in Acts 4:10, "Be it known unto you all and to all the people of Israel, that by the name of Jesus Christ of Nazareth, whom ye have crucified, whom God raised from the dead, even by Him doth this man stand here before you whole."

On several occasions when I conducted a high school assembly, I was invariably told not to say Jesus. My response was always the same, "I'll do the best I can." And my very best always meant saying Jesus. I've seen entire high schools and junior high schools repent of their sins and turn to Jesus Christ.

Most people love the name of Jesus. Don't allow political correctness to keep you from witnessing in the power of the Holy Spirit. Continue to let God anoint you to preach, teach, and speak in the name of Jesus Christ. If you do, God will immensely bless you, and Jesus will change the hearts of those you witness to. America—keep saying "Jesus!"

While I was in Singapore, I was told by a restaurant owner to quit writing the name "Jesus" on my bill. I would always leave a good tip, and was able to boldly witness to the waiters and waitresses. Many were gloriously born again. However, I would also write something about Jesus on the bill. Something like, "Jesus loves you" or "Freedom in Christ" or "Jesus is alive!" At any rate, I was given the ultimatum to not write His name. As a result, I boycotted that restaurant and refused to eat until I was allowed to write the name of Jesus. Finally, the Muslim management gave in, and I continued to be a bold witness for Christ.

Friend, don't ever let people intimidate you. If God be for us, who can be against us? The apostle John wrote, "Greater is He who is in me, that He that is in the world."

The apostle Paul confessed, "I live, yet not I but Christ liveth in me."

In John 1:12, we are promised power from God: "But as many as received Him, to them gave He power to become the sons of God, even to them that believe on His name."

We are anointed to witness. The Holy Spirit empowers us to boldly proclaim Christ. We have the Word of God, which is sharper than any two-edged sword. We have guardian angels and a mandate from God to go into all the world and preach the gospel of Jesus Christ to every person. Let's do it in Jesus' name!

Keep Going Strong for Jesus

Yes friend, the good news is that these bold men and women of God refused to quit saying Jesus. Their response to the verbal and the physical abuse is found in Acts 5:42, "And daily in the temple and in every house, they ceased not to teach and preach Jesus Christ."

The apostle Paul explained it this way in 2 Corinthians 4:3-6:

But if our gospel be hid, it is hid to them that are lost: In whom the god of this world hath blinded the minds of them which believe not, lest the light of the glorious gospel of Christ, who is the image of God, should shine unto them. For we preach not ourselves, but Christ Jesus the Lord; and ourselves your servants for Jesus sake. For God, who commanded the light to shine out darkness hath shined in our hearts to give the light of knowledge of the glory of God in the face of Jesus Christ.

Yes, the early church was verbally and physically assaulted for saying "Jesus." Down through the ages, millions of Christians were put to death for speaking the name that is above every name!

So it is today, the name of Jesus is under attack. Anyone who proclaims His name (especially in a public forum) is labeled intolerant, ignorant, narrow-minded, and bigoted. In many countries of the world, thousands of Christians are being martyred for speaking the name of Jesus. Over two million Christians in the Sudan have already died at the hands of Muslims. Nearly 340 Christians everyday die for the cause of Christ.

If the devil can keep Christians from saying "Jesus," the unsaved world will stay lost. Souls will keep going to hell, and we won't see revival and reap the harvest. We must get Jesus into our conversations.

Colossians 3:16, "Let the word of Christ dwell in you richly in all wisdom; teaching and admonishing one another in psalms and hymns and spiritual songs, singing with grace in your hearts to the Lord."

Colossians 3:17, "And whatsoever ye do in word or deed, do all in the name of the Lord Jesus, giving thanks to God and the Father by Him."

Many Christians remain quiet and passionless. Mel Gibson's boldness to speak up for Jesus Christ should challenge every believer to do the same.

L.R. Scarborough wrote:

"Remember the prize is worth the noblest effort. You deal with immortal souls, dear to God, to Christ, and to you. If I were to live a thousand years and win one soul to Christ, my life would have been immeasurably worthwhile if I did nothing else; but I should win souls everyday, whether I live long or short. If I had ten thousand lives, I would give every one of them full-length for winning souls and serving Christ."

Dr. Billy Graham is a strong advocate for Jesus Christ. Not only has he seen millions come to Christ through his ministry, but he has faithfully equipped the body of Christ to do the same.

Regarding personal witnessing, Rev. Graham said:

We should pray and work for revival, and we must also pray and work (in the words of the Affirmation) for 'a renewed dedication to the biblical priority of evangelism in the church.' God's people are called by God to do various things. We are called to worship God. We are called to teach the Word of God so that believers might be strengthened. We are called to have a social concern for those in need in our world. All of these responsibilities (and others we might mention) are legitimate and important. But the greatest responsibility—the highest priority—is evangelism, reaching a lost world for Christ.

Tragically, the church has often lost sight of this, relegating evangelism so that the biblical mandate and message are lost. We should be thankful for evidences today of a renewed commitment to evangelism by many churches—but we should also be concerned that other parts of the Body of Christ have become indifferent to the plight of the lost and have become preoccupied with internal programs. May those of us to whom God has entrusted a special ministry of evangelism be burdened for God's people, and pray and work for restoration of the biblical priority of evangelism to the church of Jesus Christ, in all of its diversity around the world.

In his book, *Soul Winning Out Where the People Are*, T.L. Osborn said the following:

We are soul winners because we have taken God's Word seriously. We do not want the blood of the unconverted to ever be required at our hands. It is as simple as that! In my estimation, the most important opportunity in the life of any Christian- not just ministers, but all Christians- is to witness to the unconverted. Christ only reached them through men and women in whom He lives. Soul winning is not a pastime or a hobby. Soul winning is Christianity in action every day. As soon as we are saved, we can share Christ with others. We are Christ's voice, His mouthpiece. If we are silent, Christ is silenced. He only speaks through us. This is not something we do when it is convenient. Soul winning is our number one priority in life- our life's greatest opportunity! Wouldn't it be wonderful if soul winning became the major theme of every Bible school, every youth group, every Sunday school, every Bible conference and convention?

Charles Finney, like Billy Graham, shook America for Jesus Christ. As a lawyer, Dr. Finney emphasized the importance of sharing Jesus Christ. He wrote:

The city is going to hell. Yes, the world is going to hell and will continue to do so until the church finds out how to win souls. The best-educated ministers are those who win the most souls. It is the great commission of every Christian to save souls. Now, if you are neglecting the main business of life, what are you living for?

What constitutes the spirit of prayer? Is it many prayers and warm words? No. Prayer is the state of the heart. The spirit of prayer is a state of continual desire and anxiety for the salvation of sinners. A Christian who has this spirit of prayer feels anxious for souls. They are always on his mind. He thinks of them by day and dreams of them by night. This is "praying without ceasing." His prayers seem to flow from his heart like water.

When sinners are careless and stupid, it is time for Christians to get to work. It is as much their duty to wake up, as it is a fireman to wake up when a fire breaks out. The church must put out the fires of hell that are consuming the wicked. Sleep? Should the fireman sleep and let the whole city burn down? What would people think of such a fireman? And yet the guilt of Christians who sleep while sinners around them are sinking into the fires of hell.

What else would you live for than to save souls? Would you not rather save souls than be President of the United States?

What do you propose to do, young man, or young woman, with your education? Have you any higher or nobler object to live for than to save souls? Have you any more worthy object upon which to expend the resources of a cultivated mind and the accumulated powers gained by education? Think—what should I live for but the gems of heaven- for what but the honor of Jesus, my Master?

They who do not practically make the salvation of souls—for their own and others—their chief concern, deserve not the name of rational; they are not sane. Look at their course of practical life as compared with their knowledge of facts. Are they sane, or are they deranged?

It is time for the church to consecrate her mind and her whole heart to this subject. It is indeed time that she should lay these great truths in all their burning power close to her heart. Alas, how is her soul palsied with the spirit of the world! Nothing can save her and restore her to spiritual life until she brings her mind and heart into burning contact with these living, energizing truths of eternity.

The church of our time needs the apostolic spirit. She needs so deep a baptism which those fires of the Holy Ghost that she can go out and set the world on fire by her zeal for the souls of men. Till then the generation of our race must go on, thronging the broad way to hell because no man cares for their souls.

Preaching Jesus is the Father's business.

Winning souls is God's business. The Father had one Son and He made Him a soul winner. Jesus didn't just win souls; He died for lost humanity to be saved. Everything Jesus did was to bring men into the kingdom of God, to reconcile mankind back to the Father. Throughout the life of Christ we find Jesus is either talking to man about God or talking to God about man.

At the age of twelve, we find Jesus sharing the gospel. Then later at the age of thirty until He died, all Jesus did was witness about His power, talk of His Father, and demonstrate God's love. Jesus casted out devils, healed the sick, and took authority over religious hypocrisy. It's probably safe to say, that even as Jesus labored as a carpenter, He was also laboring to win His fellow friends.

The gospel message is simple, "For God so loved the world that He gave His only begotten Son, that whosoever believeth in Him should not perish but have everlasting life. For God sent not His Son into the world to condemn the world, but that the world through Him might be saved" (John 3:16-17).

Jesus made it clear that we all have a choice; it's heaven or hell. Christ said, "Verily, verily, I say unto thee, except a man be born again, he cannot see the kingdom of God" (John 3:3).

The apostle Paul spoke of it in 2 Corinthians 5:17, "Therefore if any man be in Christ, he is a new creature: old things are passed away; behold all things are become new."

This born-again experience is not an option but a necessity to become a citizen in the kingdom of God, and is only found in Jesus Christ. John 14:6 quotes our Lord, "I am the Way, the Truth, and the Life: no man cometh unto the Father, but by me."

The Father's business is the process of getting people to accept Jesus Christ, which in turn reunites them to the Father, by the power of the Holy Spirit.

Jesus taught that we must repent or perish (Luke 13:3). The apostle Peter wrote, "The Lord is not slack concerning his promise, as some men count slackness; but is longsuffering to us-ward, not willing that any should perish, but that all should come to repentance" (2 Peter 3:9).

Romans 3:23 says, "For all have sinned and come short of the glory of God." Sin separates us from the Father and keeps us out of heaven. That's why we must accept Jesus Christ—who knew no sin as our Savior, "whose blood cleanseth us from all sin" (1 John 1:7). Romans 6:23 teaches, "For the wages of sin is death; but the gift of God is eternal life through Jesus Christ our Lord."

This act of repentance must also be accompanied by faith. Each person must believe that God sent Jesus and that in Christ he or she is a new person. Romans 10:9-10 promises, "That if thou shalt confess with thy mouth the Lord Jesus, and shalt believe in thine heart that God has raised Him from the dead, thou shalt be saved. For with the heart man believeth unto righteousness; and with the mouth confession is made unto salvation."

Faith via repentance brings us to God, and faith in God overcomes the world. The apostle John wrote, "For whatsoever is born of God overcometh the world, even our faith."

Not only does faith and repentance go together but likewise you will find believing and receiving as interrelated. John 1:12 explains, "But as many as received him, to them gave he power to become the sons of God, even to them that believe on His name." Jesus clarified this even further in Revelation 3:20, "Behold, I stand at the door, and knock: if any man hear my voice, and open the door, I will come in to him, and will sup with him, and he with me."

Now many will come to the conclusion that a person must earn this privilege. Thus religion was started. However, salvation is called a gift, and no merit on our part is needed. Paul wrote in Ephesians 2:7-9, "That in the ages to come He might shew the exceeding riches of His grace in His kindness toward us through Christ Jesus. For by grace are ye saved through faith; and that not of yourselves; it is the gift of God. Not of works, lest any man should boast."

Galatians 2:16 teaches, "Knowing that a man is not justified by the works of the law, but by the faith of Jesus Christ, even we have believed in Jesus Christ, that we might be justified by the faith of Christ, and not by the works of the law: for by the works of the law shall no flesh be saved."

As a matter of fact, Scripture teaches that our righteousness is but filthy rags to God (Isaiah 64:6). In other words, no person will ever be good enough for heaven in his own flesh. All have sinned, and without Christ as our only mediator to God, we will never be born again.

You see, "the scripture hath concluded all under sin, that the promise by faith of Jesus Christ might be given to them that believe. But before faith came, we were kept under the law, shut up unto faith which should afterwards be revealed. Wherefore the law was our schoolmaster to bring us unto Christ, that we might be justified by faith. But after faith is come, we are no longer under a schoolmaster. For ye are all the children of God by faith in Christ Jesus" (Galatians 3:22-26).

Now after we believe on Christ, God gives us Holy Ghost power to live the Christian life. However, scripture makes it plain, we can't live the Christian life or abide by the law of God apart from faith in Christ.

Galatians 3:10-14 says:

For as many as are of the works of the law are under the curse; for it is written, cursed is everyone that continueth not in all things which are written in the book of the law to do them. But that no man is justified by the law in the sight of God, it is evident, the just shall live by faith. And the law is not of faith: but, the man that doeth them shall live in them. Christ hath redeemed us from the curse of the law, being made a curse for us: for it is written, cursed is everyone that hangeth on a tree: That the blessing of Abraham might come on the Gentiles through Jesus Christ; that we might receive the promise of the Spirit through faith.

Thus, the Father's business is getting people to have this personal experience with God, through faith in Jesus Christ which comes via repentance of sin, confessing with one's own mouth, believing in one's own heart, and finally, receiving Jesus into one's life. Paul wrote in Galatians 2:20, "I live; yet not I, but Christ liveth in me."

When you are born again, Jesus comes into your heart and body via the Holy Spirit. "The Spirit itself beareth witness with our spirit, that we are children of God" (Romans 8:16).

The Holy Spirit is given to all believers to empower us to live for God (John 1:12). The baptism of the Holy Spirit is given to us for witnessing. The Holy Spirit is the evidence that you have been born again. In Romans 8:9-11, Paul wrote, "But ye are not in the flesh, but in the Spirit, if so be that the Spirit of God dwell in you. Now if any man have not the spirit of Christ, he is none of this. And if Christ be in you, the body is dead because of sin; but the Spirit is life because of righteousness. But if the Spirit of Him that raised up Jesus from the dead dwell in you, he that raised up Christ from the dead shall also quicken your mortal bodies by his Spirit that dwelleth in you."

The good news is, salvation is a free gift. The gift is an eternal life insurance policy, where the premiums have been paid by Jesus Christ. He forgives us our sins, gives us eternal life (heaven), and gives us Holy Ghost power. That is the Father's business: it's the greatest business on the face of the earth.

John spoke of it, "Ye are of God, little children, and have overcome them; because greater is He that is in you, than he that is in the world" (1 John 4:4).

Paul summed it up when he said, "O death, where is thy sting? O grave where is thy victory? The sting of death is sin; and the strength of sin is the law. But thanks be to God, which giveth us the victory through our Lord Jesus Christ" (1 Corinthians 15:55-57).

Should we be about the Father's business? Jesus said, "As the Father has sent me, so I send you" (John 20:21)!

The Pressure to Conform

The prophet Micah was encouraged via intimidation and conformity to prophesy that good thing which all the prophets had already spoken to the king. However, Micah couldn't be bought. We read his statement of independence from man and dependence on God alone: "As the Lord liveth, even what my God saith, that will I speak."

It's not always easy being a prophet, especially when your words don't conform, nor confirm the words of the false prophets. When your words seem hard, tough, and negative, you are oftentimes cast aside as an undesirable. The prophet Micah was put in prison.

Peter was also imprisoned for preaching repentance. As an angel of the Lord delivered him and officers found him once again preaching the cross and resurrection of Jesus, the high priest asked Peter and the others, "Did not we straitly command you that ye should not teach in this name? and behold, ye have filled Jerusalem with your doctrine, and intend to bring this man's blood upon us" (Acts 5:28).

The natural man would say Peter was stubborn, or narrow-minded, or even rebellious. Some would even suggest that Peter was careless, irresponsible, and insensitive to those Christians who were trying to be accepted by society. Yet, Peter and the other apostles would not conform to the pressure of their peers. Just like the prophets before them and just like Jesus their Savior, they made their life's decision plain, and boldly said, "We ought to obey God rather than men" (Acts 5:29).

This statement is the foundation of discipleship, sanctification, and the Spirit-filled life. This is the difference between real champions for God and halfhearted backsliders. This is the difference between contenders and those just pretending. Jesus put it another way: "How can you receive honor from God, when you seek honor from each other?" Again, our Lord spoke in Luke 16:15, "For that which is highly esteemed among men is an abomination in the sight of God."

As Christians we must decide who our master will be. Jesus said, "Ye cannot serve two masters." We cannot serve people and God, nor can we serve pleasure and God, nor money and God. It must be God and God alone. Joshua made his decision very clear, "As for me and my house, we shall serve the Lord" (Joshua 24:15).

What is your decision? Will you serve God or mammon? Is it Christ or this world's glory? Moses chose God even at the expense of human glory and fleshly lusts.

"Choosing rather to suffer affliction with the people of God than to enjoy the pleasure of sin for a season. Esteeming the reproach of Christ greater riches than the treasures in Egypt: for he had respect unto recompence of that reward" (Hebrews 11:25,26).

Like Joshua, Moses would not conform to world opinion. Instead, he made a quality decision to please God. Today the pharaohs of Egypt are largely forgotten, and they burn in hell this very hour. Yet, Moses lives now in heaven, and even his earthly name is mentioned daily all across this world. Moses gave up temporary glory for eternal glory. He gave up immediate satisfaction for everlasting peace. He gave up earthly fame for a heavenly crown.

How about you? Do you have Jesus? Are your sins forgiven? Young man, young woman, today is the day of salvation. Jesus said, "Ye must be born again" (John 3:3). "[Unless] ye repent, ye likewise will perish" (Luke 13:3). Christ reiterated, "For what shall it profit a man, if he shall gain the whole world and lose his own soul?" (Mark 8:36).

The world is building its hopes and dreams on sand. Jesus said when the storm comes, these homes will crumble and be destroyed. But Christ promised that he who builds his house—or life—upon the Rock, Christ, his house shall be solid and shall never fall.

Don't let man's opinions or your personal sins keep you out of heaven. Repent right now and invite Jesus Christ into your life. If you're already a Christian, start witnessing for Christ. Don't go along with the crowds of backsliders who care little for the saving of a lost humanity. You, be different! Be what God called you to be. Be a witness for His power and soon-coming. Don't settle for second best. Be something special for God. Don't worry about your dreams. Be the dream. Be God's dream.

Together we can make the difference. Let's win lost souls to Jesus. Let us work while it is yet day. Let us be about the Father's business.

Compare Jesus, the Savior of the world to the founders of other religions:

Jesus never sinned.

The rest of the so-called prophets admitted to many of their own sins.

Jesus lived and promoted love.

Many of the others promoted hate, violence, deceit and murder to establish their religions.

Jesus lived as a celibate.

Muhammad had ten wives and Joseph Smith had at least thirty-seven.

Jesus was born of a virgin. His Father was God.

All other prophets were born of earthly parents.

Jesus was constantly working miracles.

The other prophets never performed even one miracle.

Jesus healed all diseases.

The other prophets healed no one.

Jesus rose again as an empty tomb lay in Israel.

All the other prophets died as mere humans and their grave sights are evident in different parts of the world.

Jesus was a fulfillment of prophesies.

The other prophets were only a fulfillment of their own dreams.

Jesus lived and died for people.

The other prophets lived and died for their own causes.

Jesus was the only prophet that claimed to be God.

All the others were men.

Jesus proved His God-power by His fulfillment of prophecy, His virgin birth, His miracles, His sinless life, His teachings, His extreme intelligence, His perfection, His love, His insight, and by His death and resurrection. The wind and seas obeyed him, and the demons obeyed Him.

The other prophets proved their frail humanity by their failures, their sins, their deceit, their hate, and many by the murders they oversaw.

All other religious leaders needed Jesus to save them from their own sin.

Jesus Christ is the Savior of the world and the only way to Heaven.

Martin Luther wrote, "Take hold of Jesus as a man and you will discover that He is God. To the hurting, He is the great Physician. To the confused, He is the Light. To the lost, He is the Way. To the hungry, He is the Bread of Life. To the thirsty, He is the Water of Life. To the broken, He is the Balm in Gilead."

Calvin Miller- "Christ's humanity is the great hem of the garment, through which we can touch His Godhead."

"I confess Jesus Christ, the Son of God with my whole being. Those whom you call gods are idols; they are made by hands." –Said by Alban, first British martyr, when asked to offer sacrifices to the gods Jupiter and Apollo.

Philip Schalf, a well-respected historian wrote:

"This Jesus of Nazareth, without money and arms, conquered more millions than Alexander, Caesar, Muhammad, and Napoleon; without science... He shed more light on things human and divine than all philosophers and scholars combined; without the eloquence of schools, He spoke such words of life as were never spoken before or since, and produced effects which lie beyond the reach of orator or poet; without writing a single line, He set more pens in motion, and furnished themes for more sermons, orations, discussions, learned volumes, works of art, and songs of praise than the whole army of great men of ancient and modern times."

J.C. Ryle wrote: "Let us serve Him faithfully as our Master. Let us obey Him loyally as our king. Let us study His teachings as our Prophet. Let us walk diligently after Him as our example. Let us look anxiously for Him as our coming Redeemer of body as well as soul. But above all let us prize Him as our sacrifice, and rest our whole weight on His death as atonement for sin. Let His blood be more precious in our eyes every year we live. Whatever else we glory in about Christ, let us glory above all things in His cross."

Jonathan Edwards, "Christ is like a river. A river is continually flowing, these are fresh supplies of water coming from the fountainhead continually, so that a man may live by it, and be supplied with water all his life. So Christ is an ever-flowing fountain; He is continually supplying His people, and the fountain is not spent. They who live upon Christ may have fresh supplies from Him to all eternity; they may have increase of blessedness that is new, and new still, and which never will come to an end."

John H. Gerstner, "To the artist He is the one altogether lovely. To the educator He is the master teacher. To the philosopher He is the wisdom of God. To the lonely He is a brother; to the sorrowful, a comforter; to the bereaved, the resurrection and the life, and to the sinner He is the Lamb of God who takes away the sin of the world."

Desiderius Eramus, "By a carpenter the world was made, and only by the carpenter can mankind be remade."

Oscar Pfister, "Tell me the picture of Jesus you have reached and I will tell you some important facts of your nature."

Patrick Henry, "It cannot be emphasized too often or too strongly that this great nation was founded not by religionists but by Christians; not on religions but on the gospel of Jesus Christ..."

Woodrow Wilson, "A man has deprived himself of the best that is in the world who has deprived himself of this Bible."

John Bacon, "What can I do with respect to the next world without my Bible"?

Daniel Webster, "The Bible is the book of faith and a book of doctrine, a book of morals, a special revelation of God."

Immanuel Kant, "The Bible is the greatest benefit which the human race has ever experienced."

Galileo, "I believe that the intention of the Holy writ was to persuade men of the truths necessary to salvation."

Read the following declaration...

"We the undersigned, students of Natural Science, desire to express sincere regret that researchers into scientific truth are perverted by some in our own times into occasion for casting doubt upon the truth and authenticity of the Holy Scriptures. We conceive that it is impossible for the Word of God written in the book of nature, and God's Word written in Holy Scripture, to contradict one another, physical science is not complete, but it is only in condition of progress."

Thomas Jefferson, "I hold the precepts of Jesus as delivered by Himself, to be the most pure, benevolent and sublime which have ever been preached to man..."

John Paul II, "The whole of Christ's life was a continual teaching: His silences, His miracles, His gestures, His prayer, His love for people, His special affection for the little and the poor, His acceptance of the total sacrifice on the cross for the redemption of the world, and His resurrection are the actualization of the word and the fulfillment of revelation."

Thomas Brooks, "He is a portion that exactly, and directly suits, the condition of the soul, the desires of the soul, the necessities of the soul, the wants of the soul, the longings of the soul, and the prayers of the soul. The soul can crave nothing, nor wish for nothing, but what is to be found in Christ. He is the light to enlighten the soul, wisdom to counsel the soul, power to support the soul, goodness to supply the soul, mercy to pardon the soul, beauty to delight the soul, glory to ravish the soul, and fullness to fill the soul."

John Flavel, "Christ is the very essence of all delights and pleasures, the very soul and substance of them. As all the rivers are gathered in the ocean, which is the meeting place of all the waters in the world, so Christ is the ocean in which all true delights and pleasures meet."

Napoleon wrote, "Christ alone has succeeded in so raising the mind of man towards the unseen that it becomes insensible to the barriers of time and space."

H.A. Ironside, "Christ is a substitute for everything, but nothing is a substitute for Christ."

Martin Luther wrote, "When Jesus Christ utters a word, He opens his mouth so wide that it embraces all heaven and earth, even though that word be but a whisper." He also said, "Either sin is with you, lying on your shoulders, or it is lying on Christ, the Lamb of God. Now if it is lying on your back you are lost; but if it is resting on Christ, you are free, and you will be saved. Now choose what you want." At another time, he wrote, "In his life Christ is an example, showing us how to live; in His death He is a sacrifice, satisfying for our sins; in His resurrection, a conqueror; in His intercession, a high priest."

S.D. Gordon said, "Jesus was God spelling Himself out in a language humanity could understand."

Kenneth Scott Latourette, "As the centuries pass the evidence is accumulating that, measured by His effect on history, Jesus is the most influential life ever lived on this planet."

The good mathematician Blaise Pascal said, "Knowledge without Jesus Christ is useless and barren."

The famous Prime minister of Britain confessed, "All that I live for is based on the divinity of Christ."

C.S. Lewis, one of the great intellectual giants of the twentieth century said, "God has landed on this enemy-occupied world in human form. The perfect surrender and humiliation was undergone by Christ... perfect because He was God."

The well-known American statesman, Daniel Webster, proclaimed, "I believe Jesus Christ to be the Son of God."

The Apostle's Creed, which was written around AD 100, states, "I believe in God the Father Almighty, Maker of heaven and earth and in Jesus Christ, His only Son, our Lord."

Then later, the Nicene Creed was written to correct some false doctrine. The Nicene Creed was written by the Father of the Christian faith around AD 325. It clearly states, "I believe in one Lord Jesus Christ, the only begotten Son of God being of one substance with the Father."

To get quotes even earlier, we must turn to Ignatius who died in AD 110. Ignatius was the leader and spokesmen for the Antioch Church. This great man of God was martyred in the Colosseum. He lived at the time of Polycarp, who himself was a disciple of John. Ignatius wrote to the Christians at Ephesus and said, "Jesus Christ our God, by the blood of God, who is God in man, for our God, Jesus the Christ and Jesus Christ, our God" (all quotations found from his epistles to the Ephesians, chapters 1-3).

Then there was a man who led the church after Ignatius. Irenaeus (AD 125-200) was a disciple of Polycarp. Irenaeus wrote in *Against Heresies* (4:10) how Christ was often seen by Moses, and that it was Christ who spoke from the burning bush.

Another contemporary Bible scholar Justin Martyr (A.D. 110-166) wrote, "Our Christ conversed with Moses under the appearance of fire from a bush." It was not the Father of the universe who thus spoke to Moses, but "Jesus the Christ," "the Angel and Apostle" who is also GOD, yea "the God of Abraham, Isaac and Jacob," "the I AM that I AM."

Ladies and gentlemen, God chose that the fullness of the Godhead bodily is found in Jesus Christ. That's why the apostle Paul gives us this warning in Colossians 2:8-10, "Beware lest any man spoil you through philosophy and vain deceit after the tradition of men, after the rudiments of the world and not after Christ. For in Him dwelleth all the fullness of the Godhead bodily. And ye are complete in Him, which is the head of all principality and power."

Jesus Christ deserves to be proclaimed!

- He was born of a virgin.
- He was a seed planted by the Holy Spirit.
- He said before Abraham was "I AM."
- He lived a perfect, sinless life.
- He died on the cross for our sins.
- He arose triumphantly on the third day.
- He ascended into Heaven and sat down at the right hand of God.
- He is the Creator of all things visible and invisible.
- His blood atones for our sin.
- His Holy Spirit gives us power to live for God.
- He will return to the earth again as King of Kings and Lord of Lords.

So, **America Say "Jesus!"**

Yes, friend, there is power in the name of Jesus. Say His name everyday to every person you meet. Say His name when you pray. Pray for and encourage our President and other leaders to say His name publicly. We must define the name of the God of America. And His name is Jesus Christ. Our founding fathers served Him and founded this nation on His name and the Word of God.

Abraham Lincoln, "All the good from the Saviour of the world is communicated through this Book; but for the Book we could not know right from wrong. All the things desirable to man are contained in it."

Woodrow Wilson, "... the Bible ... is the one supreme source of revelation of the meaning of life, the nature of God and spiritual nature and need of men. It is the only guide of life which really leads the spirit in the way of peace and salvation."

Andrew Jackson, "Go to the Scriptures... the joyful promises it contains will be a balsam to all your troubles."

Calvin Coolidge, "The foundations of our society and our government rest so much on the teachings of the Bible that it would be difficult to support them if faith in these teachings would cease to be practically universal in our country."

First John 5:13, "These things have I written unto you that believe on the name of the Son of God, that ye may know that ye have eternal life, and that ye may believe on the name of the Son of God."

Robert E. Lee urged all Americans to pray for our country, our families and all of those who do not know Jesus Christ: "Knowing that intercessory prayer is our mightiest weapon and the supreme call for all Christians today, I pleadingly urge our people everywhere to pray. Believing that prayer is the greatest contribution that our people can make in this critical hour, I humbly urge that we take time to pray—to really pray. Let there be prayer at sunup, at noonday, at sundown, at midnight—all through the day. Let us all pray for our children, our youth, our aged, our pastors, our homes. Let us pray for our churches. Let us pray for ourselves, that we may not lose the word 'concern' out of our Christian vocabulary. Let us pray for our nation. Let us pray for those who have never known Jesus Christ and redeeming love, for moral forces everywhere, for our national leaders. Let prayer be our passion. Let prayer be our practice."

Peter Marshall gave Americans this powerful challenge, "The choice before us is plain, Christ or chaos, conviction or compromise, discipline or disintegration. I am rather tired of hearing about our rights and privileges as American citizens. The time is come, it is now, when we ought to hear about the duties and responsibilities of our citizenship. America's future depends upon her accepting and demonstrating God's government."

Listen to this incredible confessions by John Newton, "I am persuaded, a broken and a contrite spirit, a conviction of our vileness and nothingness, connected with a cordial acceptance of Jesus as revealed in the Gospel, is the highest attainment we can reach in this life."

Colossians 1:15, "[Christ] He is the image of the invisible God, the first-born over all creation."

Hebrews 1:3, "The Son is the radiance of God's glory and the exact representation of his being, sustaining all things by his powerful word. After he had provided purification for sins, he sat down at the right hand of the Majesty in heaven."

Ladies and gentlemen, Jesus Christ is the Savior of the world, our personal Lord and the God of our founding fathers. His name must be proclaimed.

On July 4, 1837, President John Quincy Adams said, "Why is it that, next to the birthday of the Savior of the world, your most joyous and most venerated festival returns on this day? Is it not that, in the chain of human events, the birthday of the nation is indissolubly linked with the birthday of the Savior? That it forms a leading event in the progress of the gospel dispensation? Is it not the Declaration of Independence first organized the social compact on the foundation of the Redeemer's mission upon earth?"

Ladies and gentlemen, Jesus Christ is Lord. In Him we move, live, and have our being. Honor His name, pray in His name and proclaim His name to the ends of the earth. There is power in His name, healing and deliverance in His name and Salvation in His name!

America Say "Jesus!"

FIVE

Say Jesus...Because

(A verse-by-verse assessment of His Name)

Some of the following statements are quoted word for word from the King James Version. Other statements are summaries of what the verses mean. The purpose is to see and understand why we need to say the name that is above every name—Jesus!

This study begins with the book of Romans. I wanted to start with a book that teaches the deep doctrines of Christ. From Romans we go in chronological order through the book of Revelation. You will discover Jesus in the book of Acts and then onto special overviews in the gospels. I'm sure you will discover, as I have, the incredible power in the name and life of Christ.

ROMANS:
1. We are servants of Christ (1:1)
2. We are separated unto the gospel of God (1:1)
3. Jesus Christ is our Lord (1:3)
4. Jesus is the Son of God with power (1:4)
5. Jesus Christ was resurrected from the dead (1:4)
6. Jesus has given us grace and apostleship for His name (1:5)
7. We are called by Jesus Christ (1:6)
8. We are called to be saints (1:7)
9. Grace and peace is in Jesus Christ (1:7)
10. We are debtors to preach the gospel (1:14,15)

11. We are not ashamed of the gospel of Christ (1:16)
12. God shall judge the secrets of men by Jesus Christ (2:16)
13. The righteousness of God is by faith in Jesus Christ unto all and upon all them that believe (3:22)
14. Because all have sinned and come short of the glory of God (3:23)
15. We are justified freely by His grace through the redemption of Jesus Christ (3:24)
16. We receive our propitiation through faith in His blood to declare His righteousness for the remission of sins that are past (3:25)
17. We must declare His righteousness (3:26)
18. Because God justifies those that believe in Jesus Christ (3:26)
19. Our righteousness was imputed to us through Jesus Christ (4:23)
20. Because we believe Jesus our Lord was risen from the dead (4:24)
21. Because Jesus was delivered for our offences (4:25)
22. Because Jesus was raised for our justification (4:25)
23. Because we are justified by faith (5:1)
24. Because we have peace with God through our Lord Jesus Christ (5:1)
25. Because we have access by faith into His grace (5:2)
26. Because in Jesus we rejoice in the hope of the glory of God (5:2)
27. Because Christ died for the ungodly (5:6)
28. Christ died for us while we were yet sinners (5:8)
29. Because we are justified by His blood (5:9)
30. Because we shall be saved from wrath through Him (5:9)
31. We have been reconciled to God by the death of His son (5:10)
32. We have been saved by His life (5:10)
33. Because our joy in God is through our Lord Jesus Christ (5:11)
34. Because we have now received the atonement in Jesus Christ (5:11)
35. We have received the free gift by God's grace in Jesus Christ hath abounded unto many (5:15)
36. The free gift of Christ brings justification (5:16)

37. Because we shall reign in life by one, Jesus Christ through His abundance of grace (5:17)
38. Because God's grace will reign through righteousness unto eternal life by Jesus Christ our Lord (5:21)
39. We were baptized into Christ's death (6:3)
40. Because like Christ, who was raised from the dead, so we should walk in newness of life (6:4)
41. We have been planted into the likeness of His death (6:5)
42. We will also be in the likeness of His resurrection (6:5)
43. Our old man is crucified with Christ (6:6)
44. Because we should not serve sin (6:6)
45. Because we shall live with Christ (6:8)
46. Because Christ was raised from the dead; death hath no more dominion over Him (6:9)
47. Because we are dead unto sin and alive unto God through Jesus Christ our Lord (6:11)
48. Because we are free from sin and are servants of God (6:22)
49. Because we have fruit unto holiness and everlasting life (6:22)
50. Because the gift of God is eternal life through Jesus Christ our Lord (6:23)
51. We are dead to the law by the body of Christ (7:4)
52. We are delivered from the law (7:6)
53. There is no condemnation to them which are in Christ Jesus (8:1)
54. The Spirit of the life of Christ hath made me free from the law of sin and death (8:2)
55. Jesus Christ condemned sin in the flesh (8:3)
56. When Christ is in us, the body is dead because of sin (8:10)
57. But the spirit is life because of righteousness (8:10)
58. Because Christ is risen from the dead, your mortal bodies shall be quickened by His Spirit that dwelleth in you (8:11)
59. We are joint-heirs with Christ (8:17)
60. If we suffer with Christ, we will be glorified together (8:17)
61. Jesus Christ maketh intercession for the saints according to the will of God (8:27)
62. We are predestined to be conformed to the image of Jesus Christ (8:29)
63. Jesus Christ was delivered up for us all, therefore God will with Him freely give us all things (8:32)

64. Christ died, is risen again, and is at the right hand of God who also maketh intercession for us (8:34)
65. Nothing shall separate us from Christ (8:35-39)
66. We are more than conquerors through Christ who loves us (8:37)
67. We should speak the truth in Christ (9:1)
68. Christ came, who is over all, God blessed forever (9:5)
69. That the name of God and His power will be declared throughout all the earth (9:17)
70. Christ is the end of the law for righteousness to everyone that believeth (10:4)
71. If we confess with our mouth the Lord Jesus, and shall believe in thine heart that God hath raised Him from the dead thou shalt be saved (10:9)
72. For whosoever shall call upon the name of the Lord shall be saved (10:13)
73. We are one body in Christ and every one members one of another (12:5)
74. We should put on the Lord Jesus Christ and make not provision for the flesh, to fulfill the lusts thereof (13:14)
75. We should regard each day unto the Lord (14:6)
76. We live unto the Lord (14:8)
77. Because Jesus is Lord both of the dead and the living (14:9)
78. Because we shall stand before the judgment seat of Christ (14:10)
79. Because every knee shall bow and every tongue shall confess to God (14:11)
80. Because we shall give an account of ourselves to God (14:12)
81. I know and am persuaded by the Lord Jesus Christ that there is nothing unclean of itself (14:14)
82. The kingdom of God is not meat and drink; but righteousness peace and joy in the Holy Ghost. For he that in these things serveth Christ is acceptable to God and approved of men (14:17-18)
83. For even Christ pleased not Himself (15:3)
84. We should be like-minded one toward another according to Christ Jesus (15:5)
85. So that we will glorify God, even the Father of our Lord Jesus Christ (15:6)

86.   Because Christ has received us unto the glory of God (15:7)
87.   Because Jesus Christ confirms the promises of God (15:8)
88.   Because we are ministers of Jesus Christ (15:8)
89.   That we may glorify God for His mercy (15:9)
90.   Because we are ministers for Jesus Christ (15:16)
91.   That I may glory through Jesus Christ (15:17)
92.   So I will fully preach the gospel of Jesus Christ (15:19)
93.   Now I beseech you brethren for the Lord Jesus Christ's sake (15:30)
94.   The grace of our Lord Jesus Christ be with you (16:20)
95.   Because Jesus Christ has the power to establish you in the gospel (16:25)
96.   Because the revelation of Jesus Christ was kept a mystery since the world began (16:25)
97.   Because God receives the glory through Jesus Christ (16:27)

1 CORINTHIANS

98.   Because we are called by Jesus Christ through the will of God (1:1)
99.   We are sanctified in Christ (1:2)
100.   We are called to be saints (1:2)
101.   In every place we call upon the name of Jesus Christ our Lord (1:2)
102.   Grace and peace from God our Father and from the Lord Jesus Christ (1:3)
103.   Because we are enriched by Christ in all utterance and in all knowledge (1:5)
104.   Because the testimony of Christ is confirmed in you (1:6)
105.   Because we're waiting for the coming of our Lord Jesus Christ (1:7)
106.   Because we are confirmed unto the end that we may be blameless in the day of our Lord Jesus Christ (1:8)
107.   We have been called into fellowship of His Son Jesus Christ our Lord (1:9)
108.   That we should all speak the same thing and be of the same mind because of the name of our Lord Jesus Christ (1:10)
109.   Jesus sent us to preach the gospel (1:17)
110.   Because the preaching of the cross is the power of God (1:18)
111.   We preach Christ crucified (1:23)

112.   Jesus Christ is the power of God and the wisdom of God (1:24)
113.   Because we are in Christ Jesus (1:30)
114.   Because Christ is made unto us wisdom, righteousness, sanctification, and redemption (1:30)
115.   Because we are determined to know nothing among you save Jesus Christ and Him crucified (2:2)
116.   Jesus is the only foundation (3:11)
117.   We are Christ's and Christ is God's (3:23)
118.   We are the ministers of Christ (4:1)
119.   He that judgeth me is the Lord (4:4)
120.   Jesus will bring to light the hidden things of darkness (4:5)
121.   We are fools for Christ (4:10)
122.   We have been begotten unto the gospel through Jesus Christ (4:15)
123.   We need to know our leader's ways which be in Christ (4:17)
124.   We have power in our Lord Jesus Christ (5:4)
125.   There is coming a judgment day by Christ (5:5)
126.   Christ has been sacrificed for us (5:7)
127.   In Christ we are washed (6:11)
128.   Justified in the name of the Lord Jesus and by the Spirit of God (6:11)
129.   Because God raised up the Lord and will also raise up us by His own power (6:14)
130.   Our bodies are the members of Christ (6:15)
131.   Because we are in Christ and by Him (8:6)
132.   Because not every man has the knowledge (8:7)
133.   The spiritual Rock is Christ (10:4)
134.   We should not tempt Christ (10:9)
135.   The cup of blessing which we bless, is it not the communion of the blood of Christ (10:16)
136.   We are also all partakers of that one bread (10:17)
137.   We do not want to provoke the Lord to jealousy (10:22)
138.   For the earth is the Lord's and the fullness thereof (10:26)
139.   Even as I please all men in all things, not seeking mine own profit, but the profit of many, that they may be saved (10:33)
140.   We are to be followers of Jesus Christ (11:1)
141.   The head of every man is Christ (11:3)

142. For as often as ye eat this bread and drink this cup, ye do shew the Lord's death till He come (11:26)
143. No man can say Jesus is Lord but by the Holy Ghost (12:3)
144. Now ye are the body of Christ and members in particular (12:27)
145. Because Christ died for our sins (15:3)
146. Because Christ rose again on the third day (15:4)
147. Because over five hundred witnesses saw Christ after his resurrection (15:5,6)
148. Because Jesus rose from the dead and is the firstfruits of them that slept (15:20)
149. In Christ we shall be made alive (15:22)
150. We are Christ's at His coming (15:23)
151. Christ will reign and have put all things under His feet (15:25-27)
152. All things shall be subdued by Christ (15:28)
153. Because Christ Himself shall be subject unto the Father (15:28)
154. Because God the Father put all things under Jesus Christ (15:28)
155. That God the Father may be our all in all (15:28)
156. We need to die everyday in Christ Jesus (15:31)
157. Because the first man is of the earth, earthy: the second man is the Lord from heaven (15:47)
158. But thanks be to God, which giveth us the victory through our Lord Jesus Christ (15:57)
159. Always work for Jesus for your labor is not in vain (15:58)
160. If any man love not the Lord Jesus Christ, let him be Anathema Maranatha (15:58)
161. The grace of our Lord Jesus Christ be with you (16:23)
162. My love be with you all in Christ Jesus. Amen. (16:24)

2 CORINTHIANS
163. Grace and Peace from our Lord Jesus Christ (1:2)
164. Our consolation aboundeth by Christ (1:5)
165. We should rejoice as ye are also in the family of God on the day of our Lord Jesus (1:14)
166. Because Jesus Christ is the Son of God (1:19)
167. Because all the promises of God are in Jesus Christ (1:20)

168. Because we are established in Christ (1:21).
169. We forgive each other in the person of Christ (2:10)
170. Christ opens the door to preach the gospel (2:12)
171. We triumph in Christ (2:14)
172. God maketh manifest the savour of His knowledge by us in every place (2:14)
173. For we are unto God a sweet savour of Christ (2:15)
174. Because out of sincerity we speak of Christ (2:17)
175. We are made effective ministers of the new testament (3:6)
176. The old testament veil is done away in Christ (3:14)
177. Where the spirit of the Lord is, there is liberty (3:17)
178. As we behold the Lord, we are changed into the same image from glory to glory, even as by the Spirit of the Lord (3:18)
179. But if our gospel be hid, it is hid to them that are lost (4:3)
180. Our goal is that the light of the glorious gospel of Christ, who is the image of God, should shine unto lost sinners (4:4)
181. God has shined in our hearts, to give the light of the knowledge of the glory of God in the face of Jesus Christ (4:6)
182. Always bearing about in the body the dying of the Lord Jesus, that the life also of Jesus might be made manifest in our body (4:10)
183. We are delivered unto death for Jesus' sake, that the life also of Jesus might be made manifest in out mortal flesh (4:11)
184. Knowing that He which raised up the Lord Jesus shall raise up us also by Jesus and shall present us with you (4:14)
185. Wherefore we labour, that whether present or absent, we may be accepted of Him (5:9)
186. For we must all appear before the judgment seat of Christ (5:10)
187. Knowing therefore the terror of the Lord, we persuade men (5:11)
188. For the love of Christ constraineth us (5:14)
189. If any man be in Christ, he is a new creature (5:17)
190. God hath reconciled us to Himself by Jesus Christ (5:18)
191. God was in Christ, reconciling the world unto Himself (5:19)
192. We are ambassadors for Christ (5:20)
193. Jesus who knew no sin, became sin for us that we might be made the righteousness of God in Him (5:21)

194. For ye know the grace of our Lord Jesus Christ, that though He was rich, yet for your sakes He became poor, that ye through His poverty might be rich (8:9)

195. We are to be messengers of the church for the glory of Christ (8:23)

196. Now I Paul myself beseech you by the meekness and gentleness of Christ (10:1)

197. We should bring every thought to the obedience of Christ (10:5)

198. But he that glorieth, let him glory in the Lord (10:17)

199. Because we want to be presented as a chaste virgin to Christ (11:2)

200. Because our minds are not corrupted from the simplicity that is in Christ (11:3)

201. Jesus said "My grace is sufficient for thee: for my strength is made perfect in weakness (12:9)

202. When we are weak in our flesh, then are we strong in Christ (12:10)

203. We speak for before God in Christ (12:19)

204. Because Jesus was crucified through the weakness yet He liveth by the power of God toward you (13:4)

205. Jesus Christ is in you (13:5)

206. The grace of the Lord Jesus Christ and the love of God and the communion of the Holy Ghost be with you all. Amen. (13:14)

GALATIANS

207. God raised Jesus from the dead (1:1)

208. Jesus gave Himself for our sins (1:4)

209. That He would deliver us from this present evil world (1:4)

210. To please God is to be a servant of Jesus Christ (1:10)

211. The gospel is taught by the revelation of Jesus Christ (1:12)

212. God wants to reveal His Son Jesus Christ in us (1:16)

213. We have liberty in Christ Jesus (2:4)

214. That the truth of the gospel of Christ will continue in you (2:5)

215. We are justified by the faith of Jesus Christ (2:16)

216. Because we are crucified with Christ (2:20)

217. Christ has redeemed us from the curse of the law (3:13)

218. The blessing of Abraham comes on us through Jesus Christ (3:14)
219. That we might receive the promise of the Spirit by faith (3:14)
220. The covenant was confirmed before of God in Christ (3:17)
221. Because the Bible says all is under sin (3:22)
222. That the promise by faith of Jesus Christ might be given to them that believe (3:22)
223. The law was our schoolmaster to bring us unto Christ (3:24)
224. We are the children of God by faith in Jesus Christ (3:26)
225. For we who have been baptized unto Christ have put on Christ (3:27)
226. For ye are all one in Christ Jesus (3:28)
227. In Christ we are Abraham's seed and heirs according to the promise (3:29)
228. God sent forth His Son, made of a woman, made under the law (4:4)
229. To redeem them that were under the law, that we might receive the adoption of sons (4:5)
230. And because you are sons, God hath sent forth the Spirit of His Son into your hearts, crying Abba, Father (4:6)
231. Because Christ has made us free (5:1)
232. Because Jesus Christ is our righteousness by faith (5:5)
233. And they that are Christ's have crucified the flesh the affections and lusts (5:24)
234. Bear ye one another's burdens and so fulfill the law of Christ (6:2)
235. Because we only glory in the cross of Jesus Christ (6:14)
236. In Christ, we are a new creation (6:15)

EPHESIANS

237. We are blessed by Jesus Christ with all spiritual blessings in heavenly places in Christ (1:3)
238. We are chosen in Christ before the foundation of the world (1:4)
239. We are predestined and adopted by Jesus Christ (1:5)
240. We are accepted into the beloved of Christ (1:6)
241. We have redemption through His blood (1:7)
242. The forgiveness of sins according to His grace (1:7)

243. Because Christ hath abounded toward us in all wisdom and providence (1:8)
244. Jesus hath made known unto us the mystery of His will (1:9)
245. That in the dispensation of the fullness of times, He might gather together in one all things in Christ (1:10)
246. Because in Christ we have an inheritance (1:11)
247. Because by trusting in Christ, we should be to the praise of His glory (1:12)
248. Because Jesus is the Word of truth (1:13)
249. After we believed in Christ we are sealed with that Holy Spirit of promise (1:13)
250. We are Christ's redemption of His purchased possession (1:14)
251. In Christ, we have received the Spirit of wisdom and revelation in the knowledge of Him (1:17)
252. By Christ resurrection, we can know the hope of his calling (1:18)
253. The riches of the glory of the inheritance (1:18)
254. The exceeding greatness of His power (1:19)
255. Which He wrought in Christ and set Him at His own right hand in heavenly places (1:20)
256. Far above principality and power and might and dominion and every name that is named not only in this world, but also in that which is to come (1:21)
257. Because all things are under His feet and He is over all things to the church (1:22)
258. Because in Christ we find fullness because He fills our all in all (1:23)
259. We are quickened together with Christ (2:5)
260. We are raised up together and are sitting together in heavenly places in Christ Jesus (2:6)
261. Because in Christ we will know the exceeding riches of His grace in His kindness toward us in Christ Jesus (2:7)
262. Because we are saved by grace (2:8)
263. We are His workmanship created in Christ Jesus (2:10)
264. In Christ we have hope, a promise and God in this world (2:12)
265. In Jesus we are made nigh by his blood (2:13)
266. He is our peace, there is no partition between us (2:14)

267. Christ hath abolished in His flesh, the enmity, the law of the commandments to make us a new man (2:15)
268. By the cross of Christ, He has slain the enmity thereby (2:16)
269. In Christ we have access by one spirit unto the Father (2:18)
270. Because we are no longer strangers and foreigners, but fellow citizens with the saints and household of God (2:19)
271. Jesus Christ is the chief corner stone (2:20)
272. God created all things by Jesus Christ (3:9)
273. The eternal purpose of God is revealed in Jesus Christ (3:11)
274. In Christ we have boldness and access by the faith of Him (3:12)
275. Because Jesus is worthy for us to bow and to worship God (3:14)
276. In Jesus the whole family in heaven and earth is named (3:15)
277. In Jesus you can be strengthened with might by His Spirit in the inner man (3:16)
278. Because Christ dwells in our hearts by faith (3:17)
279. That in Jesus we can be rooted and grounded in love (3:17)
280. That in Christ we can comprehend and know the love of Christ that passeth knowledge (3:18-19)
281. Because in Christ He is able to do exceedingly abundantly above all that we ask or think (3:20)
282. Because Jesus is worthy to receive glory in the church throughout all ages world without end. Amen (3:21)
283. We are given grace according to the measure of the gift of Christ (4:7)
284. Because genuine ministry edifies the body of Christ (4:12)
285. Our goal is to come in unity of the faith and the knowledge of the Son of God, unto a perfect man, unto the measure of the stature of the fullness of Christ (4:32)
286. Because Christ is the head of the church (4:15)
287. The truth is in Jesus (4:21)
288. Because God for Christ sake hath forgiven us (4:13)
289. Because Jesus hath loved us and hath given Himself for us as an offering and a sacrifice to God for a sweet smelling savour (5:2)
290. Awake thou that sleepest and arise from the dead and Christ shall give thee light (5:14)
291. Giving thanks in the name of our Lord Jesus Christ (5:20)

292. Christ is the head of the Church and He is the Saviour of the body (5:23)
293. Because the church is subject unto Christ (5:24)
294. Christ loved the church and gave Himself for it (5:25)
295. That He might sanctify and cleanse it with the washing of water by the word (5:26)
296. That He might present it to Himself a glorious Church, not having spot or wrinkle or any such thing; but that it should be holy and without blemish (5:27)
297. Jesus Christ nourisheth and cherisheth the Church (5:29)
298. This is a great mystery: but I speak concerning Christ and the Church (5:32)
299. With singleness of heart do your job faithfully as unto Christ, Not with eyeservice, as menpleasers; but as the servants of Christ, doing the will of God from the heart (6:5,6)
300. With good will doing service as to the Lord and not to men (6:7)
301. Knowing that whatsoever good thing any man doeth, the same shall he receive of the Lord (6:8)
302. Be strong in Christ and in the power of His might (6:10)
303. And for me, that utterance may be given unto me, that I may open my mouth boldly to make known the mystery of the gospel (6:19)
304. For which I am an ambassador in bonds: that I may speak boldly as I ought to speak (6:20)
305. Peace and love with faith from God the Father and the Lord Jesus Christ (6:23)
306. Grace be with all them that love our Lord Jesus Christ in sincerity. Amen. (6:24)

PHILIPPIANS

307. Because we are servants of Jesus Christ, because we are in Christ and have received His grace and peace from God the Father (1:1-2)
308. Because our fellowship is in the gospel of Jesus Christ (1:5)
309. Because Jesus will finish the good work that He started in you and will perform it until the day of Jesus (1:6)
310. Because we are partakers of His grace (1:7)

311. Because we want to be sincere and without offence till the day of Jesus (1:10)

312. Because in Christ we have been filled with the fruits of righteousness which are by Jesus Christ, unto the glory and praise of God (1:11)

313. That no matter what happens in our lives we should help further the gospel of Christ (1:12)

314. Because we should speak the word of God without fear (1:14)

315. Because we rejoice when Christ is preached (1:18)

316. Because with boldness we want Christ Jesus to be magnified in our body (1:20)

317. To live is Christ, and to die is gain (1:21)

318. We should let our conversation be as it becometh the gospel of Christ (1:27)

319. We should with one mind strive together for the faith of the gospel (1:27)

320. Because we are given on behalf of Christ not only to believe on Him, but also to suffer for His sake (1:29)

321. Jesus Christ humbled Himself unto the death of the cross, but God hath highly exalted Him, and given Him a name which is above every name (2:8-9)

322. At the name of Jesus, every knee shall bow and every tongue shall confess the Jesus Christ is Lord, to the glory of God the Father (2:11)

323. We need to hold forth the Word of life that we may rejoice in the day of Christ (2:16)

324. We rejoice in Christ Jesus (3:3)

325. Our desire is the knowledge of Christ (3:8)

326. That we may please Christ (3:8)

327. And be found in Christ (3:9)

328. That I may know Him and the power of His resurrection and the fellowship of His sufferings (3:10)

329. I press toward the mark for the prize of the high calling of God in Christ Jesus (3:14)

330. Our conversation is in heaven (3:20)

331. Heaven, where we look for the Savior, the Lord Jesus Christ (3:20)

332. Jesus shall change our vile body to be like His (3:21)

333. And He shall subdue all things unto Himself (3:21)
334. God's peace keeps our hearts and minds through Jesus Christ (4:7)
335. We can do all things through Christ (4:13)
336. God shall supply all our needs according to His riches in glory by Christ Jesus (4:19)
337. The grace of Jesus Christ shall be with you. Amen (4:23)

COLOSSIANS

338. Our hope in heaven is sure (1:5)
339. Our gospel is in the word of truth (1:5)
340. The gospel produces fruit in us (1:6)
341. That ye might walk worthy of the Lord unto all pleasing, being fruitful in every good work and increasing in the knowledge of God (1:10)
342. Strengthened with all might, according to His glorious power, unto all patience and longsuffering with joyfulness (1:11)
343. We have been delivered from the power of darkness (1:13)
344. We have been translated into the Kingdom of His dear Son (1:13)
345. We have redemption through His blood and the forgiveness of sins (1:14)
346. Jesus is the image of the invisible God and the firstborn of every creature (1:15)
347. All things were created by and for Him (1:16)
348. Jesus is before all things and by Him all things consist (1:17)
349. Jesus is the head of the body, the church (1:18)
350. That Jesus would have preeminence in all things (1:18)
351. In Christ all the fullness dwells (1:19)
352. We have peace through the blood of the cross (1:20)
353. All things are to be reconciled unto Jesus (1:20)
354. And we are reconciled to Christ (1:21)
355. Jesus will present us holy, unblameable, and unreproveable in His sight (1:22)
356. Christ in us is the hope of glory (1:27)
357. We preach and warn every man that we may present everyman perfect in Jesus Christ (1:28)

358. Their people's hearts will be comforted in their understanding of God the Father and of Christ (2:2)
359. In Jesus, are hid all the treasures of wisdom and knowledge (2:3)
360. We are rooted and built up and established in the faith by Jesus Christ (2:7)
361. In Christ dwells all of the Godhead bodily (2:9)
362. We are complete in Christ who is the head of all principalities and power (2:10)
363. We are buried with Christ in baptism and we are risen with Him through the faith of the operation of God who hath raised Him from the dead (2:12)
364. We have been quickened by Christ and forgiven our trespasses (2:13)
365. Jesus has blotted out the ordinances that were against us and that were contrary and nailed them to the cross (2:14)
366. Jesus has spoiled principalities and power. He made a shew of them openly, triumphing over them in it (2:15)
367. We are risen with Christ (3:1)
368. Jesus is seated at the right hand of God (3:1)
369. We are dead and our life is hid with Christ in God (3:3)
370. Jesus is our life (3:4)
371. Christ will appear and we shall appear with Him (3:4)
372. The Word of Christ dwells in us (3:16)
373. We are to do everything in the name of the Lord Jesus, giving thanks to God and the Father by Him (3:17)
374. Jesus will give us the reward of the inheritance (3:24)
375. We need to speak the mystery of Christ (4:3)
376. Take heed to the ministry which you have received of the Lord that you fulfill it (4:17)

1 THESSALONIANS
377. We need to have the patience of our hope which is in our Lord Jesus Christ (1:3)
378. Jesus will return from heaven (1:10)
379. God raised Jesus from the dead (1:10)
380. Jesus delivered us from the wrath to come (1:10)
381. Jesus Christ is coming again (2:19)

382. You are our hope, joy and crown of rejoicing at the coming of our Lord Jesus Christ (2:19)
383. We are fellow labourers in the gospel of Christ (3:2)
384. Now God Himself and our Father and our Lord Jesus Christ, direct our way unto you (3:11)
385. Jesus will make you to increase and abound in love one to another (3:12)
386. Christ will establish our hearts unblameable in holiness before God (3:13)
387. Jesus Christ will return with His saints (3:13)
388. We exhort each other by Jesus Christ (4:1)
389. We believe that Jesus died and rose again (4:14)
390. The Lord Himself shall descend from Heaven (4:16)
391. We which are alive and remain shall be caught up together to meet the Lord in the air (4:17)
392. We shall forever be with the Lord (4:17)
393. Jesus will come as a thief in the night (5:2)
394. God has delivered us from wrath in Christ (5:9)
395. We have obtained salvation by our Lord Jesus Christ (5:9)
396. We will live together with Christ (5:10)
397. In everything give thanks for this is the will of God in Christ Jesus concerning you (5:18)
398. God will preserve you blameless unto the coming of our Lord Jesus Christ (5:23)
399. The grace of our Lord Jesus Christ be with you (5:28)

2 THESSALONIANS

400. Grace and Peace from God the Father and our Lord Jesus Christ (1:2)
401. Jesus will be revealed from heaven with His mighty angels (1:7)
402. Jesus will take vengeance on them that know not God and that obey not the gospel of our Lord Jesus Christ (1:8)
403. Jesus will punish the unbeliever with everlasting destruction from the presence of the Lord and from the glory of His power (1:9)
404. Jesus will come to be glorified in His saints (1:10)
405. God wants the name of Jesus Christ to be glorified in us (1:12)

406. Jesus is coming and we shall be gathered together unto Him (2:1)
407. The day of Christ is at hand (2:2)
408. Jesus shall consume the wicked and shall destroy him with the brightness of His coming (2:8)
409. God called us via the gospel to the obtaining of the glory by our Lord Jesus Christ (2:14)
410. Jesus has given us (because of His love), everlasting consolation and good hope through grace (2:16)
411. The Lord Jesus is faithful who shall stablish you and keep you from evil (3:3)
412. We are patiently waiting for Christ (3:5)
413. We should, in the name of our Lord Jesus Christ withdraw ourselves from every brother that walks disorderly (3:6)
414. That Jesus, who is Peace, will give you peace always by all means (3:16)
415. The Grace of our Lord Jesus Christ be with you all (3:18)

1 TIMOTHY

416. Jesus Christ is our hope (1:1)
417. Grace, mercy and peace from God the Father and our Lord Jesus Christ (1:2)
418. Jesus Christ enables us and puts us in the ministry (1:12)
419. The grace of Christ is exceedingly abundant: Jesus Christ came into the world to save sinners (1:14-15)
420. In Jesus Christ, life is everlasting (1:16)
421. Jesus Christ is King eternal, immortal, invisible, the only wise God (1:17)
422. Jesus Christ is the only mediator between God and men (2:5)
423. Christ gave Himself as a ransom for all (2:6)
424. We should have great boldness in the faith which is in Christ Jesus (3:13)
425. God was manifest in the flesh, justified in the spirit, seen of angels, preached unto the Gentiles, believed on the word, received up into glory (3:16)
426. We need to be good ministers of Jesus Christ (4:6)
427. We both labour and suffer reproach because we trust in

the living God, who is the Saviour of all men, specially of those that believe (4:10)

428. We are changed before God and the Lord Jesus Christ that we do things without preferring one before another, doing nothing by partiality (5:21)

429. We need to consent to wholesome words, even the words of our Lord Jesus Christ (6:3)

430. The doctrine of our Lord Jesus Christ is according to godliness and we are to keep this commandment without spot, unrebukeable until the appearing of our Lord Jesus Christ (6:1-14)

2 TIMOTHY

431. We have the promise of life in Jesus Christ (1:1)

432. Grace, mercy and peace is in God the Father and our Lord Jesus Christ (1:2)

433. Be not ashamed of the testimony of our Lord Jesus Christ (1:8)

434. Jesus hath saved us and called us with a holy calling (1:9)

435. Jesus has abolished death and hath brought life and immortality to light through the gospel (1:10)

436. For I know whom I have believed and am persuaded that He is able to keep that which I have committed unto Him against that day (1:12)

437. Hold fast the form of sound words, which thou hast heard of me, in faith and love which is in Christ Jesus (1:13)

438. We are to be strong in the grace of Jesus Christ (2:1)

439. We are to be a good soldier of Jesus Christ (2:3)

440. Jesus Christ was raised from the dead (2:8)

441. We want people to obtain the salvation which is in Christ Jesus with eternal glory (2:10)

442. If we are dead with Christ, we shall also live with Him (2:11)

443. Let every one that nameth the name of Christ depart from iniquity (2:19)

444. All who live godly in Christ Jesus shall suffer persecution (3:12)

445. The Bible is able to make you wise unto salvation through faith in Jesus Christ (3:15)

446. Jesus Christ shall judge the quick and the dead at His appearing and His Kingdom (4:1)

447. Everyone who knows Christ and loved His appearing will receive a crown of righteousness (4:8)
448. The Lord will stand with His ministers and strengthen them to preach the gospel of Christ (4:17)
449. We shall be preserved unto Christ's heavenly Kingdom to whom be the glory for ever and ever (4:18)

TITUS
450. He is our hope of eternal life (1:2)
451. Jesus commanded that His word be manifested through preaching (1:3)
452. Grace, mercy, and peace comes from God the Father and the Lord Jesus Christ our Savior (1:4)
453. The grace of God that bringeth salvation hath appeared to all men (2:11)
454. We are looking for that blessed hope and the glorious appearing of the great God and our Savior Jesus Christ (2:13)
455. Jesus gave Himself for us, that He might redeem us from all iniquity and purify unto Himself a peculiar people, zealous of good works (2:14)
456. The kindness and love of God our Savior toward man has appeared (3:4)
457. Jesus saved us by His mercy, by the washing of regeneration and renewing of the Holy Ghost (3:5)
458. This mercy has been shed on us abundantly through Jesus Christ our Savior (3:6)
459. We are justified by his grace (3:7)
460. We should be made heirs according to the hope of eternal life (3:7)

PHILEMON
461. We are a fellow laborer with Jesus Christ (1:1)
462. The communication of thy faith may become effectual by the acknowledging of every good thing which is in you in Christ Jesus (1:6)
463. The grace of our Lord Jesus Christ be with your spirit. Amen. (1:25)

HEBREWS

464. God hath in these last days spoken unto us by His Son, whom He hath appointed heirs of all things by whom also He made the worlds (1:2)

465. Jesus is the brightness of God's glory (1:3)

466. Jesus is the express image of His person (1:3)

467. The upholding of all things by the word of His power (1:3)

468. Jesus has purged our sins and has sat down on the right hand of the Majesty on high (1:3)

469. Jesus is made so much better than the angels, as he hath by inheritance obtained a more excellent name than they (1:4)

470. Jesus was begotten of the Father (1:5)

471. Thy throne (Jesus the Son of God) o God, is forever and ever, a sceptre of righteousness is the sceptre of thy Kingdom (1:8)

472. Jesus in the beginning hast laid the foundation of the earth; and the heavens are the works of thy hands (1:10)

473. Thou madest him a little lower than the angels; thou crownedst Him with glory and honor and didst set Him over the works of thy hands (2:7)

474. Thou hath put all things in subjection under His feet (2:8)

475. Jesus suffered unto death, was crowned with glory and honor that He, by the grace of God should taste death for every man (2:9)

476. By Jesus are all things and by whom are all things in bringing many sons unto glory to make the captain of their salvation perfect through sufferings (2:10)

477. His name is declared and praised in the church (2:12)

478. Through the death of Jesus He has destroyed the devil (2:14)

479. Jesus hath delivered us from bondage because of the fear of death (2:15)

480. Jesus is a faithful and a merciful high priest in things pertaining to God, to make reconciliation for the sins of the people (2:17)

481. Jesus is able to succour them that are tempted (2:18)

482. Jesus is the High Priest of our profession (3:1)

483. Jesus was counted worthy of more glory than Moses (3:3)

484. Jesus built all things (3:4)

485. Jesus is passed into the heavens (4:14)
486. Jesus is the author of eternal salvation unto all them that obey Him (5:9)
487. Jesus is the anchor of the soul, both sure and steadfast (6:19)
488. Jesus was made a surety of a better testament (7:22)
489. Jesus has an unchangeable priest hood (7:24)
490. Jesus is able to save them to the uttermost (7:25)
491. Jesus even liveth to make intercession for us (7:25)
492. Jesus is holy, harmless, undefiled, separated from sin, and made higher than the heavens (7:26)
493. Jesus is consecrated for evermore (7:28)
494. Jesus is the high priest set on the right hand of the throne of the Majesty in the heavens (8:1)
495. Jesus is the minister of the sanctuary (8:2)
496. Jesus is the mediator of a better covenant, which was established upon better promises (8:6)
497. Jesus by His own blood entered in once into the holy place, having obtained eternal redemption for us (9:12)
498. Jesus, by His blood, has purged your conscience from dead works to serve the living God (9:14)
499. Jesus is the mediator of the new testament that we might receive the promise of eternal inheritance (9:15)
500. Jesus is in heaven to appear in the presence of God for us (9:24)
501. Jesus offered to bear the sins of man (9:28)
502. Jesus shall appear the second time without sin unto salvation (9:28)
503. We are sanctified through the offering of His body (10:10)
504. Jesus is set down on the right hand of God (10:12)
505. From henceforth expecting till His enemies be made His foot stool (10:13)
506. Jesus was raised from the dead by God (11:19)
507. Jesus is the author and finisher of our faith (12:2)
508. Jesus endured the cross, despising the shame, and is set down at the right hand of the throne of God (12:2)
509. Jesus resisted unto blood, striving against sin (12:4)
510. Jesus is the mediator of the new covenant (12:24)
511. Jesus says "I will never leave thee nor forsake thee" (13:5)
512. Jesus is the same yesterday, today, and forever (13:8)

513. Jesus sanctifies the people with His own blood (13:12)
514. Jesus was brought again from the dead; is the Great Shepherd of the sheep through the blood of His everlasting covenant (13:20)

JAMES
515. Jesus will give the crown of life the Lord has promised to them that love Him (1:12)
516. Jesus is the Lord of Glory (2:1)
517. Jesus is able to save and destroy; He is the only lawgiver (4:12)
518. Jesus will receive the early and the latter rain (5:7)
519. The coming of the Lord draweth nigh (5:8)
520. In the name of the Lord Jesus (when a person is anointed with oil by an elder) that the prayer of faith is made, Jesus will then raise Him up and forgive him of his sins (5:14-15)

1 PETER
521. We have a lively hope by the resurrection of Jesus Christ from the dead (1:3)
522. We have an inheritance, incorruptible and undefiled and that fadeth not away, reserved in heaven for you (1:4)
523. Jesus Christ is the end of our faith, even the salvation of our souls (1:9)
524. Hope to the end for the grace that is to be brought unto you at the revelation of Jesus Christ (1:13)
525. He is the Lamb without blemish and without spot (1:19)
526. He was foreordained before the foundation of the world, but was manifest in these last times for you (1:20)
527. God raised Him from the dead (1:21)
528. We are born again of an incorruptible seed, by the word of God, which liveth and abideth forever (1:23)
529. Jesus is a living stone, disallowed of men, but chosen of God and is precious (2:4)
530. In Christ we will not be confounded (2:6)
531. He is the head of the corner (He is the cornerstone) (2:7)
532. He is a stone of stumbling and a rock of offense (2:8)
533. We are a chosen generation, a royal priesthood, a holy nation, a peculiar people that we should shew forth praises unto Him who hath called us out of darkness into light (2:9)

534. Jesus suffered for us and we should follow in His steps (2:21)
535. He did not sin, neither was guile found in His mouth (2:22)
536. Who in His own self bare our sins in His own body on the tree (2:24)
537. By His stripes we are healed (2:24)
538. He is the Shepherd and the Bishop of our souls (2:25)
539. Jesus suffered once for sins, the just for the unjust, that he might bring us to God, being put to death in the flesh but quickened by the Spirit (3:18)
540. He is gone into heaven and is on the right hand of God, angels and authorities and power made subject unto Him (3:22)
541. He will judge the quick and the dead (4:5)
542. That God in all things may be glorified through Jesus Christ to whom be praise and dominion forever and ever. Amen. (4:11)
543. His glory shall be revealed (4:13)
544. We are called by the God of all grace unto eternal glory by Christ Jesus (5:10)
545. To Him be glory and dominion forever and ever (5:11)

2 PETER
546. The righteousness of God is in Jesus Christ (1:1)
547. Grace and Peace is multiplied through the knowledge of God and of Jesus our Lord (1:2)
548. His divine power hath given unto us all things that pertain unto life and godliness (1:3)
549. We are to be fruitful in the knowledge of our Lord and Savior Jesus Christ (1:8)
550. Our Lord Jesus Christ has an everlasting kingdom (1:11)
551. He received from God the Father honor and glory saying, 'This is my beloved Son, in whom I am well pleased' (1:17)
552. The long suffering of our Lord is salvation (3:15)
553. We are to grow in grace and in the knowledge of our Lord and Savior Jesus Christ. To Him be glory both now and forever. Amen. (3:18)

1 JOHN
554. He is the word of life from the beginning (1:1)

555. His life was manifested which is eternal life (1:2)
556. Our fellowship is with the Father and with His Son Jesus Christ (1:3)
557. As we walk in the light, as He is in the light, we have fellowship one with another and the blood of Jesus Christ His Son cleanseth us from all sins (1:7)
558. Jesus Christ the righteous is our advocate with the Father (2:1)
559. He is the propitiation for our sins and the sins of the whole world (2:2)
560. Our sins are forgiven for His name sake (2:12)
561. If we acknowledged the Son, we also have the Father (2:23)
562. He hath given us the promise of eternal life (2:25)
563. So we shall not be ashamed before Him at His coming (2:28)
564. He was manifested to take away our sins and in Him is no sin (3:5)
565. Jesus laid down His life for us (3:16)
566. We should believe in the name of His Son Jesus Christ (3:23)
567. Jesus Christ gives us the Holy Spirit (3:24)
568. Greater is Jesus Christ who is in us than he who is in the world (4:4)
569. God sent His only begotten Son into the world that we might live through Him (4:9)
570. God sent His Son to be the propitiation for our sins (4:10)
571. The Father sent the Son to be the Savior of the world (4:14)
572. Whoever shall confess that Jesus is the son of God, God dwelleth in Him and He in God (4:15)
573. We love Him, because He first loved us (4:19)
574. Whosoever believeth that Jesus is the Christ is born of God (5:1)
574. Everyone who believes that Jesus is the Son of God overcometh the world (5:5)
576. Jesus Christ came by water and by blood which is witnessed by the Spirit of God which is truth (5:6)
577. Jesus Christ is the witness of God which He testified in His Son (5:9)
578. Eternal life is given by God through His Son (5:11)
579. He that hath the Son, hath life and he that hath not the Son hath not life (5:12)

580. We can know we have eternal life because we believe on the name of the Son of God (5:13)

581. We can know Him that is true and we are in Him that is true, even in His Son Jesus Christ. This is the true God, and eternal life (5:20)

2 JOHN

582. The truth of Christ is in us and will be forever (1:2)

583. Grace, mercy and peace via God the Father and from His Son, the Lord Jesus Christ (1:3)

584. Whoever abides in the doctrine of Christ, hath both the Father and the Son (1:9)

3 JOHN

585. For the Name of Christ we go and share the gospel (1:7)

JUDE

586. We are preserved in Jesus Christ (1:1)

587. We are to look for the mercy of our Lord Jesus Christ unto eternal life (1:21)

588. Jesus is able to keep you from falling and to present you faultless before the presence of His glory with joy (1:24)

589. To the only wise God our Savior be glory and majesty, dominion and power, both now and forever. Amen (1:25)

REVELATION

590. The Revelation of Jesus Christ reveals unto us things which must shortly come to pass (1:1)

591. John bare record of the Word of God and of the testimony of Jesus Christ (1:2)

592. Grace be unto you from Jesus Christ which is and which was and which is to come (1:4)

593. Jesus is the faithful witness (1:5)

594. The first begotten of the dead (1:5)

595. The prince of the Kings of the earth (1:5)

596. Jesus loves us (1:5)

597. He washed us from our sins in His own blood (1:5)

598. He made us kings and priests unto God and His Father (1:6)

599. He cometh with clouds and every eye shall see Him (1:7)
600. Jesus is the Alpha and Omega, the beginning and the ending, which was and which is to come, the Almighty (1:8)
601. He is the one who liveth and was dead and behold He is alive forever more (1:17-18)
602. He has the keys of hell and of death (1:18)
603. If we overcome, Jesus will let us eat of the tree of life which is in the midst of the paradise of God (2:7)
604. Be faithful unto death and Jesus will give you a crown of life (2:10)
605. If you overcome, Jesus will let you eat of the hidden manna and a white stone, and in the stone a new name written (2:17)
606. Jesus shall rule the nations with a rod of iron, as the vessels of a potter shall they be broken to shivers, even as I have received of my Father and I will give him the morning star (2:27-28)
607. He that overcomes, Jesus will confess His name before the Father and before His angels (3:5)
608. Jesus will keep us from the hour of temptation (3:10)
609. Jesus will come quickly (3:11)
610. He that overcometh, Jesus will make a pillar in the temple of God (3:12)
611. If you are lukewarm, Jesus will spue you out of His mouth (3:16)
612. Jesus stands at the door and knocks, if any man hear His voice and opens the door, Jesus will come in and have fellowship with Him (3:20)
613. He that overcometh, Jesus will grant that you sit with Christ on His throne (3:21)
614. Jesus is worthy to receive glory and honour and power for Thou hast created all things and for Thy pleasure they are and were created (4:11)
615. Jesus is worthy to open the Book (5:2)
616. Jesus is the Lion of the Tribe of Judah, the root of David and Christ has prevailed to open the Book and to loose the seven seals thereof (5:5)
617. Jesus was slain and has redeemed us to God by His blood (5:9)

618. Jesus hath made us unto God, kings and priests and we shall reign on the earth (5:10)

619. Worthy is the Lamb that was slain to receive power and riches and wisdom and strength and honour and glory and blessing (5:12)

620. Blessing and honour and glory and power be unto Him that sitteth upon the throne and unto the Lamb forever and ever (5:13)

621. Jesus Christ liveth forever and ever (5:14)

622. Salvation to our God which sitteth upon the throne and unto the Lamb (7:10)

623. Amen, blessing and glory and wisdom and thanksgiving and honour and power and might be unto God forever and ever (7:12)

624. Jesus Christ the Lamb which is in the midst of the throne shall feed them and lead them unto living foundations of waters and God shall wipe away all tears from their eyes (7:17)

625. The Kingdoms of this world are become the Kingdoms of our Lord and of His Christ and He shall reign forever and ever (11:15)

626. We give thanks, O Lord God Almighty, which art and was and art to come, because Thou hast taken to Thee Thy great power and hast reigned (11:17)

627. Now is come salvation and strength and the Kingdom of God and the power of His Christ (12:10)

628. And they overcome Him by the Blood of the Lamb (12:11)

629. Worship Jesus who hast made heaven and earth and the sea and the foundations of water (14:7)

630. Great and marvelous are Thy works, Lord God Almighty; just and true are Thy ways, Thou King of the saints (15:3)

631. Jesus is holy and we should glorify His name, for all nations shall come and worship before Him, for His judgment shall be made manifest (15:4)

632. The Lord is righteous which are and was and shall be, because Thou hast judged thus (16:5)

633. The Lamb shall overcome them, because He is Lord of lords and King of kings (17:14)

634. Alleluia: salvation and glory and honour and power unto the Lord our God (19:1)

635. The Lord God omnipotent reigneth (19:6)
636. The testimony of Jesus is the Spirit of prophecy (19:10)
637. Jesus is called Faithful and True and in righteousness He doth judge and make war (19:11)
638. His name is the Word of God (19:13)
639. Out of His mouth goeth a sharp sword, that with it He should smite the nations; and Jesus shall rule them with a rod of iron; and He treadeth the winepress of the fierceness and wrath of Almighty God (19:15)
640. And He hath on His vesture and on His thigh a name written King of Kings and Lord of Lords (19:16)
641. And they lived and reigned with Christ a thousand years (20:4)
642. We shall be priests of God and of Christ and shall reign with Him a thousand years (20:6)
643. And I saw a great white throne and Him (Jesus) that sat on it from whose face the earth and the heavens fled away; and there was found no place for them (20:11)
644. And I, John, saw the Holy city, the New Jerusalem, coming down from God out of Heaven, prepared as a bride adorned for her husband (21:2)
645. Jesus will make all things new (21:5)
646. Jesus said, "It is done, I am the Alpha and Omega, The Beginning and the End. I will give unto Him that is athirst of the fountain of the water of life freely (21:6)
647. He that overcometh shall inherit all things and I will be his God and he shall be My son (21:7)
648. And I saw no temple therein; for the Lord God Almighty and the Lamb and the temple of it (21:22)
649. And the city had no need of the sun, neither of the moon, to shine in it, for the glory of God did lighten it, and the Lamb is the light thereof (21:23)
650. The only way to get into the heavenly city, is that your name must be written in the Lamb's book of life (21:27)
651. And he showed me a pure river of water of life, clear as a crystal, proceeding out of the throne of God and of the Lamb (Jesus) (22:1)
652. Jesus said, "Behold I come quickly" (22:7)

653. And my reward is with me, to give every man according as His words shall be. I am the Alpha and the Omega, the Beginning and the End, the First and the Last (22:12-13)

654. I, Jesus have sent mine angels to testify unto you these things in the church. I am the root of the offspring of David and the Bright and Morning star (22:16)

655. And the Spirit and the Bride say come and whosoever will let him take the water of life freely (22:19)

656. We should all testify, "Surely, I come quickly. Amen". Even so, come, Lord Jesus (22:20)

ACTS

657. Jesus showed Himself alive after His passion by many infallible proofs (1:3)

658. Jesus was taken up as a cloud received Him out of their sight (1:9)

659. This same Jesus, which is taken from you into Heaven, shall come again in like manner as ye have seen Him go into heaven (1:11)

660. Whosoever shall call on the name of the Lord shall be saved (2:21)

661. Jesus of Nazareth, a man approved of God among you by miracles and wonders and signs, which God did by Him in the midst of you (2:22)

662. People took Christ and by wicked hands have crucified and slain (2:23)

663. God hath raised up Jesus and loosed the pains of death (2:24)

664. Even David knew (being a prophet) that God had sworn with an oath to Him, that of the fruit of His loins, according to the flesh, He would raise up Christ to sit on His throne (2:30)

665. David was speaking of the resurrection of Christ (2:31)

666. David knowing this of Christ knew Jesus. His soul would not be left in hell, neither would his flesh see corruption (2:31)

667. This Jesus hath God raised up, whereof we all are witnesses (2:32)

668. Jesus is by the right hand of God exalted (2:33)

669. Even David said, "The Lord said unto my Lord, sit thou on my right hand (2:34)

670. Until I make thy foes thy footstool (2:35)

671. We can know with assurance that God hath made this same Jesus, whom ye crucified both Lord and Christ (2:36)

672. We all need to repent and be baptized in the name of Jesus Christ for the remission of sins and we shall receive the gift of the Holy Ghost (2:38)

673. Peter said, "In the name of Jesus Christ of Nazareth rise up and walk (3:6)

674. The God of Abraham and of Isaac and of Jacob, the God of our fathers, hath glorified His Son Jesus Christ (3:13)

675. You killed the Prince of Life, whom God hath raised from the dead, where of we are witnesses (3:15)

676. His name, through faith in his name hath made this man strong (3:16)

677. God showed by the mouth of all His prophets, that Christ should suffer He hath so fulfilled (3:18)

678. We need to repent so Jesus will blot out our sin (3:19)

679. God shall send Jesus Christ which before was preached unto you (3:20)

680. Moses said unto the fathers, a prophet shall the Lord your God raise up unto you of your brethren, like unto me, Him shall ye hear in all things whatsoever He shall say unto you (3:22)

681. God, having raised up His Son Jesus sent Him to bless you, in turning away everyone of you from his iniquities (3:26)

682. By the name of Jesus Christ of Nazareth, whom ye crucified, whom God raised from the dead, even by Him, doth this man stand before you whole (4:10)

683. This is the stone which was set at nought of you builders, which is become the head of the corner (4:11)

684. Neither is there salvation in any other; for there is none other name under heaven given among men whereby we must be saved (4:12)

685. The world sometimes threatens Christians to keep them from saying the name of Jesus (4:17)

686. And they called them, and commanded them not speak at all nor teach in the name of Jesus (4:18)

687. Jesus, Thou art God, which hast made Heaven and earth and the sea and all that is in them (4:24)

688. The Kings of the earth stood up and the rulers were gathered together against the Lord and against His Christ (4:26)

689. By stretching forth thine hand to heal and that signs and wonders may be done by the Name of the Holy Child Jesus

690. And with great power gave the apostles witness of the resurrection of the Lord Jesus and great grace was upon them (4:33)

691. They warned the apostles not to teach in the name of Jesus (5:28)

692. The God of our fathers raised up Jesus, whom ye slew and hanged on the tree (5:30)

693. Him hath God exalted with His right hand to be a Prince and a Savior, to give repentance to Israel and the forgiveness of sins (5:31)

694. They beat the apostles and commanded them not to speak in the name of Jesus (5:40)

695. The apostles rejoiced that they were counted worthy to suffer shame for the name of Jesus (5:41)

696. Everyday in the temple and in every house they continued to teach and preach Jesus Christ (5:42)

697. Heaven is my throne and the earth is my footstool (7:49)

698. Hath not my hands made all these things (7:50)

699. Stephen looked into heaven and saw the glory of God and Jesus standing on the right hand of God (7:56)

700. Behold, I see the heavens opened and the Son of man standing on the right hand of God (7:56)

701. When, Stephen was stoned he called upon God saying, "Lord Jesus, receive my spirit" (7:59)

702. Phillip went down to the city of Samaria and preached Christ unto them and many miracles occurred (8:5-7)

703. Then the people believed Phillip, preaching the things concerning the kingdom of God and the name of Jesus Christ (8:12)

704. The Holy Spirit had not come on them yet, only that they were baptized in the name of the Lord Jesus (8:16)

705. Phillip preached Jesus unto the eunuch (8:35)

706. Saying, "If thou believeth with all thine heart" and the eunuch said, "I believe that Jesus Christ is the Son of God" (8:37)

707. Saul heard from Jesus, "Saul, Saul why persecutest thou me? I am Jesus whom thou persecuted; it is hard for thee to kick against the pricks. Arise and go into the city and it shall be told thee what thou must do" (9:4-6)

708. Paul began by preaching Christ in the synagogues that He is the Son of God (9:20)

709. Paul also preached boldly in the Name of Jesus at Damascus (9:27)

710. And he spoke boldly in the Name of the Lord Jesus (9:29)

711. Peter said, "Aneas, Jesus Christ maketh thee whole; arise and make thy bed" and he arose immediately (9:34)

712. The word which God sent unto the children of Israel; preaching peace by Jesus Christ (he is Lord of Life) (10:36)

713. God anointed Jesus of Nazareth with the Holy Ghost and power; who went about doing good and healing all that were oppressed of the devil, for God was with Him (10:38)

714. We are witnesses of all things which He did both in the land of the Jews and in Jerusalem, whom they slew and hanged on a tree. Him God raised up the third day and shewed Him openly (10:39-40)

715. God commanded us to preach and to testify that Jesus was ordained by God to be the judge of the quick and dead (10:42)

716. To Him give all the prophets witness, that through His name whosoever believeth in Him shall receive the remission of sins (10:43)

717. He commanded them to be baptized in the name of the Lord (10:48)

718. The gift of the Holy Ghost is given to them who believe on the Lord Jesus Christ (11:17)

719. Through Jesus, God hath also granted the gentiles repentance unto life (11:18)

720. In Antioch they preached Jesus (11:20)

721. God according to His promise raised unto Israel a Savior, Jesus (13:23)

722. Even John the Baptist said, "Behold, there cometh one after me, whose shoes of his feet I am not worthy to loose" (13:25)

723. And whosoever feareth God is the word of salvation sent (13:26)

724. They took Jesus down from the tree and laid him in a sepulcher but God raised Him from the dead (13:29-30)

725. And many saw Him alive for many days (13:31)

726. Jesus Christ is the fulfilled promise of God in that He raised up Jesus again (13:33)

727. God said, "Thou art my Son, this day have I begotten Thee" (13:33)

728. As concerning that He raised Him up from the dead, now no more to return to corruption, He said on this wise, I will give you the same mercies of David (13:34)

729. Wherefore He saith also in another Psalm, thou shalt not suffer Thine Holy One to see corruption (13:35)

730. But He who God raised again, saw no corruption (13:37)

731. Be it known unto you therefore, men and brethren, that through this man is preached unto you the forgiveness of sins (13:38)

732. By Him all that believe are justified from all things from which ye could not be justified by the law of Moses (13:39)

733. We believe that through the grace of the Lord Jesus Christ, we shall be saved (15:11)

734. Many men have hazarded their lives for the name of our Lord Jesus Christ (15:26)

735. Paul cast the devil out of her by saying to the spirit "I command thee in the name of Jesus Christ come out of her" (16:28)

736. Believe on the Lord Jesus Christ and thou shalt be saved and thy house (16:31)

737. Christ must needs have suffered and has risen again from the dead and that this Jesus, whom I preach unto you, is Christ (17:3)

738. The Christians were accused of turning the world upside down and saying there is no King, but one King Jesus (17:6-7)

739. You can find Jesus Christ if you seek Him, for He is not far from any one of us (17:27)

740. For in Christ, we live, and move and have our being (17:28)

741. In Jesus Christ, God hath appointed a day to judge the world, in righteousness and hath given assurance unto all men, in that He hath raised Him from the dead (17:31)

742. And when they heard of the resurrection of the dead, some mocked (17:32)

743. Paul testified to the Jews that Jesus was Christ (18:5)

744. For Paul mightily convinced the Jews and that publickly shewing by the scriptures that Jesus was Christ (19:4)

745. John the Baptist said that they should believe on Him that should come after Him (which is Jesus Christ) (19:4)

746. And when they heard this, they were baptized in the name of the Lord Jesus (19:5)

747. Then certain of the vagabond Jews, exorcists, took upon them to call over them which had evil spirits, the name of the Lord Jesus, saying, 'We adjure you by Jesus whom Paul preacheth (19:13)

748. The evil spirit said, Jesus I know (even demons feared Jesus) (19:15)

749. The name of the Lord Jesus was magnified (19:17)

750. Testifying both to the Jews and also to the Greeks, repentance toward our Lord Jesus Christ (20:21)

751. Paul was willing and ready to die for the name of the Lord Jesus (21:13)

752. Paul answered "Who art Thou Lord" and he said unto me "I am Jesus of Nazareth, who thou persecuted" (22:8)

753. Paul spoke to the Sadducees and the Pharisees of the hope and resurrection of the dead (23:6)

754. Felix sent for Paul, and heard from him concerning the faith of Christ (24:24)

755. They had certain questions against him of their own superstition and of one Jesus which was dead, whom Paul affirmed to be alive (25:19)

756. Why should it be thought a thing incredible with you, that God should raise the dead (26:8)

757. Paul said, "I verily thought with myself, that I ought to do many things contrary to the name of Jesus of Nazareth (26:9)

758. At midday, Oh King, I saw in the way a light from heaven above the brightness of the sun, shining round about me (26:13)

759. And I said "Who are thou Lord?" and He said "I am Jesus whom thou persecutest (26:15)

760. But rise and stand upon thy feet for I have appeared unto thee for this purpose to make thee a minister and a witness both of these things which thou hast seen and of those things in which I will appear unto thee (26:16)

761. To open their eyes and to turn them from darkness to light and from the power of Satan unto God, that they may receive the forgiveness of sins and inheritance among them which are sanctified by faith that is in me (26:18)

762. Paul testified that Christ shall suffer and that He should be the first that should rise from the dead and should shew the light unto the people and to the Gentiles (26:23)

763. Paul expounded and testified of the Kingdom of God, persuading them concerning Jesus (28:23)

764. Preaching the Kingdom of God, and teaching those things which concern the Lord Jesus Christ (28:31)

Now, a brief summation of the Gospels

Matthew 1:18,20,21,23

765. A supernatural birth. Born as a fulfillment of prophecy (also in Matthew 2:1-23)

766. Mary was found with child of the Holy Ghost

767. An angel of the Lord appeared unto Joseph in a dream and confirmed that which is conceived in her is of the Holy Ghost

768. Jesus is His name, for He shall save His people from their sins

769. A virgin shall be with child and shall bring forth a Son and they shall call His name Emmanuel, which being interpreted is God with us

Matthew 3:11,12

770. Jesus shall baptize you with the Holy Ghost and with Fire

771. Whose fan is in His hand and He will thoroughly purge His floor and gather His wheat into the garner but He will burn up the chaff with unquenchable fire

Matthew 3:16,17

772. When Jesus was baptized in water the heavens were opened unto Him and He saw the Spirit of God descending like a dove and lightening on Him

773. A voice from heaven said, "This is my beloved Son, in whom I am well pleased"

Matthew 4:17

774. Jesus said, "Repent for the Kingdom of heaven is at hand"

Matthew 9:2-6

775. Jesus said "I have the power to forgive sins and to raise up and heal a cripple" (plus in the future verses we see Jesus even raising the dead)

Matthew 10:32,33,39

776. Whosoever therefore shall confess me before men, him will I confess before my Father which is in Heaven

777. Whosoever shall deny me before men, him will I also deny before my Father which is in heaven Jesus said, "He that findeth his life shall lose it, and he that loseth his life for my sake shall find it

Matthew 11:5,27,28

778. Jesus said (regarding His ministry) "The blind receive their sight and the lame walk, the lepers are cleansed and the deaf hear, the dead are raised up and the poor have the gospel preached unto them"

779. Jesus said "All things are delivered unto me of my Father and no man knoweth the Son but the Father, neither knoweth any man the Father save the Son and he to whosoever the Son will reveal to Him"

780. Jesus said, "Come unto me all ye that labour and are heavy laden and I will give you rest"

Matthew 12:6,8,28,40-42
781. That in this place is One greater than the temple
782. For the Son of Man is Lord even of the Sabbath day
783. Jesus said, "If I cast out devils by the Spirit of God, then the Kingdom of God is come unto you"
784. Just as Jonah was resurrected, so shall Christ be resurrected
785. Jesus is greater than Jonah
786. Jesus is greater than Solomon
787. Jesus said "before Abraham was, I am

Matthew 13:15-17, 41-44
788. Jesus walks on water
789. Those in the ship confess of a truth You are the Son of God
790. Jesus heals every person who touches Him

Matthew 15:1-39
791. Jesus calls the religious Pharisees "hypocrites"
792. Jesus explains His desire to be worshiped and explains how He knows who worships the Father because Christ came from the Father
793. Jesus describes the origin of sin and the tradition of man that bypasses the commandments of God
794. Jesus heals a daughter grievously vexed with a devil
795. Jesus heals multitudes that were lame, blind, dumb, maimed and with many other afflictions
796. Jesus was glorified as the God of Israel
797. Jesus feeds 4,000 with only seven loaves of bread and a few fish. Seven full baskets were left.

Matthew 16:15-21,24-28
798. Jesus tells Peter that the Father hast revealed unto him that Jesus is the Christ, the Son of the living God
799. Jesus tells Peter that the gates of hell cannot prevail against my church (the church of Jesus Christ)

800. Jesus tells his disciples to not tell anyone (at that time) that He was Jesus the Christ
801. Jesus tells His disciples how He must be killed and be raised again the third day
802. Jesus says He is the teacher of men unto everlasting life. If any man wants to follow Christ he must deny himself and take up his cross and follow Him
803. Jesus said, "If a man save his life he shall lose it, but whosoever shall lose his life for my sake he shall find it"
804. Jesus will come again in the glory of His Father to reward every man according to his works

Matthew 17:1-9,22,23
805. Jesus is transfigured before Peter, James, John and his brother. God the Father says, "This is my beloved Son in whom I am well pleased, hear ye Him"
806. Jesus claims He will be killed and on the third day He will rise from the dead

Matthew 18:3-19,20-35
807. Jesus warns of hell and the judgment that should come and that Christ came to save that which is lost
808. Jesus calls the God of Heaven His Father
809. Jesus speaks of power in His own name
810. Jesus teaches on the power of forgiveness and once again explains that its His heavenly Father who decides to and not to forgive according to how you forgive others

Matthew 19:28-30
811. Jesus says the day will come that the Son of Man shall sit on the throne of His glory
812. Jesus promises that everyone who hath forsaken houses or brethren or sisters or fathers or mothers or wife or children or lands for His name's sake, shall receive an hundredfold and shall inherit everlasting life

Matthew 20:18,19,22,23,28-34
813. Jesus claims in verses 1-17 to be a final say in the judgment of men and teaches men how to live

814. Jesus explains again His persecution, His betrayal, His crucifixion and resurrection
815. Again Jesus claims to be God by explaining who will sit on the right and left hand of His eternal throne
816. Jesus explains how He came to be a ransom for many
817. Jesus touches their eyes and two blind men are instantly healed

Matthew 21:1-14,18-22,31-40

818. Jesus claims to be the eternal King
819. Jesus calls the Temple of God "My house" and says "My house shall be called the house of prayer"
820. Jesus again heals the blind and the lame
821. Jesus rebukes the fig tree and it withers
822. Jesus claims to know who gets into heaven and who doesn't
823. Jesus claims to be the stone that was rejected, but has now become the head of the corner

Matthew 22:1-14,16-21,29-33,37-46

824. Jesus, being God's Son, explains what the Kingdom of Heaven is like unto
825. Jesus explains God's judgment on unrepented sinners
826. Jesus explains the importance of witnessing for His kingdom
827. Jesus shows His wisdom is divine in this life and in the life to come
828. Jesus explains the greatest of the commandments
829. Jesus again claims to be the Son of God, Lord and God in the Trinity

Matthew 24:1-51

830. Jesus prophesies His second coming and the judgment of God
831. Jesus says He will come in the clouds of heaven with power and great glory
832. Jesus says when He comes again; the world will be much like the days of Noah. Jesus said its imperative that you be ready

Matthew 25:1-12,13-46

833.   Jesus Christ foretells of His second coming and warns people to be ready

834.   Jesus explains the kingdom of Heaven and God's way of pleasing the Master

835.   Jesus talks about coming again in glory and Him sitting upon the throne of His glory

836.   Jesus explains how He will judge the nations of the world

837.   Once again Jesus refers to Himself as the everlasting King of judgment and mercy

Matthew 26:2,7,17-26

838.   Jesus predicts His betrayal and crucifixion

839.   Jesus honors the sacrificial gift of a lady and speaks as the final authority on her reward

840.   The betrayal of Jesus, a prophetic Word of Christ begins its fulfillment

841.   During the last supper, Jesus explains the power of His blood to forgive sins and the promise He gives of everlasting life

842.   Jesus predicts His own resurrection

843.   Jesus predicts the betrayal of Peter and specifically how it will happen

844.   Jesus once again speaks to His Father and accurately predicts His betrayal

845.   Jesus claims to be God's Son by saying "Thinkest not that I can now pray to my Father and He shall presently give me more than twelve legions of angels"

846.   Before the high priest, Jesus says, "Here after shall ye see the Son of Man sitting on the right hand of power and coming in clouds of Heaven"

Matthew 27:1-66

847.   The exact fulfillment of Christ betrayal

Matthew 28:1-20

848.   The specific fulfillment of Christ resurrection

849.   Jesus says "All power is given unto me in Heaven and in earth"

850.   Christ continues proving again He is God's Son, "Go ye therefore, teach all nations, baptizing them in the name of the Father and of the Son and of the Holy Ghost"

851.   And again more solid proof as Jesus promises "Teaching them to observe all things whatsoever I have commanded you and I am with you always, even unto the end of the world, amen"

Below are some other Gospel verses that prove the deity of Jesus Christ! (These are only a few samples, for clearly every verse in God's Word validates the resurrection of the living Son of God.)

More Reasons to Say Jesus, #852 to 1105

Mark
Mark 1:1,7-11,15-17
Mark 2:5-13,20,25-28
Mark 3:10-11
Mark 4:28-41
Mark 5:7-19
Mark 6:36-41,56
Mark 7:37
Mark 8:1-9,27-31,34-38
Mark 9:31,37
Mark 10:29-30,33-40,45
Mark 12:10,26-31,35-37
Mark 14:24-39
Mark 16:4-20

Luke
Luke 1:2,31-38,46-55,67-80
Luke 2:7-22
Luke 3:15-22
Luke 4:4-12,18-21,37-44
Luke 5:18-26,31-35
Luke 6:5
Luke 7:22-23
Luke 8:43-56

Luke 9:18-27,38-45,56,58-62
Luke 10:2,9,18-24
Luke 11:2-4,29-32
Luke 12:8-9,36-51
Luke 13:24-30,34-35
Luke 14:27,33
Luke 16:20-30
Luke 17:21-37
Luke 18:7-8,37-43
Luke 19:9-10,27-40,46
Luke 20:17-18,39-44
Luke 21:5-15,25-33,36
Luke 22:15-22,29-30,42-43,67-71
Luke 23:1-2,34-46
Luke 24:1-7,12-17,20-41,46-51

John
John 1:1-18,27-38,41,45-47
John 2:16-22
John 3:3-8,12-21,28-36
John 4:10,13-26,29,34-35,42,53-54
John 5:8-9,19-47
John 6:26-30,32-41,43-50,53-58,61-69
John 7:16-19,26-29,33-34,37-38,41-46
John 8:12-32,35-38,42,51,54-58
John 9:4-5,31-39
John 10:1-5,7-18,25-30,36-38
John 11:2-27,32-36,39-40
John 12:7-8,12-13,23-36,44-50
John 13:1-3,13-20,31-38
John 14:1-31
John 15:1-27
John 16:3-33
John 17:1-26
John 18:36-37
John 19:7-11
John 20:1-31
John 21:1-14,18,23-25

The name of Jesus Christ our Lord (as referring to Christ) found in the Epistles as compared to the name of God the Father and in comparison to the total number of verses in each book. Keep in mind, the Father, the Son and Holy Spirit are one.

The purpose of this is to prove that the New Testament apostles were not ashamed to say "Jesus Christ" and how Jesus Christ is the central theme of New Testament doctrine. Many other verses speak of Christ and His finished work on Calvary; however, they are not counted in the following statistics below:

Book	# of verses	The Father	The Name of Jesus
Acts	1047	235	68
Romans	432	91	61
I Corinthians	428	105	70
II Corinthians	259	67	52
Galatians	149	52	39
Ephesians	55	83	45
Philippians	104	59	40
Colossians	95	51	27
I Thessalonians	87	25	18
II Thessalonians	47	21	13
I Timothy	113	20	16
II Timothy	83	22	15
Titus	46	12	4
Philemon	25	8	8
Hebrews	303	131	23
James	108	8	2
I Peter	86	69	21
II Peter	61	26	9
I John	105	61	12
II John	13	8	4
III John	14	2	0
Jude	25	3	5
Revelation	404	175	16
Total	**4,189**	**1,334**	**568**

Note: Many references to worshiping the throne of God can be interpreted either way. However, there's only one God, so it makes no difference. The Trinity is not 1+1+1 but rather 1x1x1.

Revelation 1:11a, "Saying, I am Alpha and Omega, the first and the last."

Revelation 1:17-19, "And when I saw Him, I fell at His feet as dead. And He laid His right hand upon me, saying unto me, 'Fear not; I am the first and the last: I am He that liveth, and was dead; and behold, I am alive for evermore. Amen; and have the keys of hell and of death. Write the things which thou hast seen, and the things which are, and the things which shall be hereafter.'"

Revelation 3:5, "He that overcometh, the same shall be clothed in white raiment; and I will not blot out his name out of the book of life, but I will confess his name before my Father, and before His angels."

Revelation 3:19-22, "As many as I love, I rebuke and chasten: be zealous therefore, and repent. Behold, I stand at the door, and knock: if any man hear my voice, and open the door, I will come in to him, and will sup with him, and he with me."

Six

The Trinity

Even though this book is about the name of Jesus and the deity of Christ, I, nevertheless, believe strongly in the Trinity. I believe in God the Father, Jesus the Son, and the Holy Spirit.

Although the word "trinity" is not found in Holy Scripture, it is nevertheless referred to many times. Throughout the New Testament, you'll read about our Heavenly Father, Jesus His Son, and the Holy Spirit. All three are termed "One God." They are three separate powers, but only ONE GOD. All have uniquely different functions, but they are the same person.

The Scriptures teach that God the Father so loved the world that He gave His only begotten Son that whosoever believes in Him should not perish, but have everlasting life.

Jesus left His home in glory, was born of a virgin, lived a sinless and miraculous life, was crucified and rose again. Jesus died for our sins, and rose again to give us power over sin, death, and hell to live forever with Him in Heaven.

Yet, Christ did not leave us comfortless when he returned to Heaven. He sent the Holy Spirit to comfort us and to empower us to be His witnesses.

John 14:26-27 says, "But the Comforter, which is the Holy Ghost, whom the Father will send in my name, He shall teach you all things, and bring all things to your remembrance whatsoever I have said unto you, my peace I give unto you: not as the world giveth, give I unto you. Let not your heart be troubled, neither let it be afraid."

The Holy Spirit is a comforter. That's why there is such a peace in the born-again person's life. The Holy Spirit also empowers us. Acts 1:8, "But ye shall receive power, after that the Holy Ghost is come upon you: and ye shall be witnesses unto me both in Jerusalem, and in all Judea, and in Samaria, and unto the uttermost part of the earth."

Jesus described the Trinity when He answered Philip's questions in John 14:8, "Philip saith unto him, Lord, shew us the Father, and it sufficeth us."

And in John 14:9, "Jesus saith unto him, have I been so long time with you, and yet hast thou not known me, Philip? He that hath seen me hath seen the Father; and how sayest thou then, 'Show us the Father'?"

John 14:10, "Believest thou not that I am in the Father, and the Father in me? The words that I speak unto you I speak not of myself: but the Father that dwelleth in me, He doeth the works."

John 14:11, "Believe me that I am in the Father, and the Father in me: or else believe me for the very works' sake."

John 14:12, "Verily, verily, I say unto you, He that believeth on me, the works that I do shall he do also; and greater works than these shall he do; because I go unto my Father."

John 14:13, "And whatsoever ye shall ask in my name, that will I do, that the Father may be glorified in the Son."

John 14:14, "If ye shall ask anything in my name, I will do it."

John 14:15, "If ye love me, keep my commandments."

John 14:16, "And I will pray the Father, and He shall give you another Comforter, that He may abide with you forever;"

John 14:17, "Even the Spirit of truth; whom the world cannot receive, because it seeth Him not, neither knoweth him: but ye know him; for he dwelleth with you, and shall be in you."

John 14:18, "I will not leave you comfortless: I will come to you."

John 14:19, "Yet a little while, and the world seeth me no more; but ye see me: because I live, ye shall live also."

John 14:20, "At that day ye shall know that I am in my Father, and ye in me, and I in you."

John 14:21, "He that hath my commandments, and keepeth them, he it is that loveth me: and he that loveth me shall be loved of my Father, and I will love him, and will manifest myself to him."

Just before our Lord's ascension into Heaven, He said in Luke 24:46-49:

> And said unto them, thus it is written, and thus it behoved Christ to suffer, and to rise from 'the dead the third day: And that repentance and remission of sins should be preached in his name among all nations, beginning at Jerusalem. And ye are witnesses of these things. And behold, I send the promise of my Father upon you: but tarry up in the city of Jerusalem, until ye be endued with power from on high.

The Bible teaches that Jesus was the creator of all things visible and invisible. John wrote in John 1:1, "In the beginning was the Word, and the Word was with God, and the Word was God."

John 1:2, "The same was in the beginning with God."

John 1:3, "All things were made by Him; and without Him was not anything made that was made."

John 1:4, "In Him was life, and the life was the light of men."

John 1:5, "And the light shineth in darkness; and the darkness comprehended it not."

John 1:9, "That was the true Light, which lighteth every man that cometh into the world."

John 1:10, "He was in the world, and the world was made by Him, and the world knew Him now."

John 1:11, "He came unto His own, and His own received him not."

John 1:12, "But as many as received Him, to them gave he power to become the Sons of God, even to them that believe on His name."

John 1:13, "Which were born, not of blood, nor of the will of the flesh, nor of the will of man, but of God."

John 1:14, "And the Word was made flesh, and dwelt among us, (and we beheld His glory, the glory as the only begotten of the Father), full of grace and truth."

John 1:15, "John bare witness of him, and cried, saying, 'This was He of whom I spake, He that cometh after me is preferred before me: for He was before me"

John 1:16, "And of his fullness have all we received, and grace for grace."

John 1:17, "For the law was given by Moses, but grace and truth came by Jesus Christ."

John 1:18, "No man hath seen God at any time; the only begotten Son, which is in the bosom of the Father, He hath declared Him."

God the Father promoted Jesus and the Holy Spirit. Jesus promoted the Father and the Holy Spirit. And, the Holy Spirit promoted Jesus and the Father. This may seem a bit different, but actually the entire universe is based upon three separate functions, yet working as one. The Bible even tells us that our triune God can be understood by looking at our tri-universe as stated in Romans 1:20.

Trinity on Earth

Our universe is made up of matter, space, and time. It is all matter, all space, and all time, not portions of all three, but completely all three acting as one. Furthermore, each of these three components has three dimensions, each of which is equally significant to the importance of its function. Although space is usually accepted as one dimension, scientists substantiate the fact that it is three-dimensional. The mathematical equation is not $1+1+1=3$, but rather $1 \times 1 \times 1=1$.

Another example is that of time. Time is just one entity but comprises three important functions of divisions. Time is past, present, and future. Though all three are different, they are also the same. Time is time is time. The past is the experience of time, but no longer seen. The future is the inexperienced and unseen source of time. The present is time being revealed in the now. Each division would be totally insignificant without the other two.

Our tri-universe is actually a trinity multiplied in many various forms. Likewise, even the human being, which the Bible says was made in the image of God is triune. For example, the physical human body can be seen, heard, and touched. Each person is a soul (nature), a person (body), and a personality (spirit).

Other examples include our relationship or doctrine of proving life's various actions. Everything that happens first has a cause, then comes the event, and then comes the effects. Or, from the source to its meaning, every action of the human life always includes the motive, the act, and the purpose. Science has proven time and time again the triune universe, triune actions, and the triune human being. And within these triune examples are other triune functions. All one in purpose unified in direction and solidified in motion. If everything in life is one divided by three parts, then it proves what God said in Romans 1:20, "For the invisible things of him from the creation of the world are clearly seen, being understood by the things that are made, even his eternal power and Godhead; so that they are without excuse."

You must accept Jesus as your personal Savior, for Colossians 2:9 says, "For in him dwelleth all the fullness of the Godhead bodily."

In the first chapter of John, Jesus is called the Word of God. Now listen to the Trinity being explained in 1 John 5:5, "Who is he that overcometh the world, but he that believeth that Jesus is the Son of God?"

First John 5:6, "This is he that came by water and blood, even Jesus Christ; not by water only, but by water and blood. And it is the Spirit that beareth witness, because the Spirit is truth."

First John 5:7, "For there are three that bear record in heaven, the Father, the Word, and the Holy Ghost: and these three are one."

First John 5:8, "And there are three that bear witness in earth, the Spirit, and the water, and the blood: and these three agree in one."

First John 5:9, "If we receive the witness of men, the witness of God is greater: for this is the witness of God which he hath testified of his Son."

First John 5:10, "He that believeth on the Son of God hath the witness in himself: he that believeth not God hath made him a liar; because he believeth not the record that God gave of his Son."

First John 5:11, "And this is the record, that God hath given to us eternal life, and this life is in his Son."

First John 5:12, "He that hath the Son hath life; and he that hath not the Son of God hath not life."

First John 5:13, "These things have I written unto you that believe on the name of the Son of God; that ye may know that ye have eternal life, and that ye may believe on the name of the Son of God."

However, according to the Bible, a man or woman cannot know God the Father except they come in Jesus' name. Only in Jesus are we reconnected to the Father and only in Jesus are our sins forgiven. First John 1:9 promises, "If we confess our sins, He is faithful and just to forgive our sins and to cleanse us from all unrighteousness."

Jesus said in John 14:6, "I am the Way, the Truth and the Life, no man goeth unto the Father but by me."

The apostle Paul explains in Galatians 1:6-12 the importance of following the true gospel of Jesus Christ.

Galatians 1:6, "I marvel that ye are so soon removed from him that called you into the grace of Christ unto another gospel:"

Galatians 1:7, "Which is not another; but there be some that trouble you, and would pervert the gospel of Christ."

Galatians 1:8, "But though we, or an angel from heaven, preach any other gospel unto you than that which we have preached unto you, let him be accursed."

Galatians 1:9, "As we said before, so say I now again, if any man preach any other gospel unto you than that ye have received, let him be accursed."

Galatians 1:10, "For do I now persuade men, or God? Or do I seek to please men? For if I yet pleased men, I should not be the servant of Christ."

Galatians 1:11, "But I certify you, brethren, that the gospel which was preached of me is not after man."

Galatians 1:12, "For I neither received it of man, neither was I taught it, but by the revelation of Jesus Christ."

Yes, friend, without Jesus Christ no one can be saved or delivered by the power of God. Without Jesus, no one goes to heaven, and eternal life is unattainable. Without Jesus, no one can know God or be at peace with the Father. Without Jesus, no one will ever know the power of the resurrection, or will they ever be able to live above sin. Without Christ's blood being shed, no person would ever experience the forgiveness of sins, a clean conscience, a renewed mind, or a new spirit. Without Christ, no man or woman would ever experience the light of God and would always live in darkness. Without Christ, no one could cast out devils, or plead the blood over difficult circumstances. Without Jesus, we lose protection from our enemies. It was the blood that made the death angel pass by. Without Christ, we could never be justified, sanctified, or redeemed. Without Jesus, we could never be filled with the Holy Spirit. Therefore, without Jesus, no person could ever experience genuine love, joy, or peace. Without Christ, we never would have learned to love our enemies and to pray for those who despitefully wrong us. Without Christ, we could never believe God for the supernatural. There would have been no walking on the water, healing the sick, raising the dead, or multiplying the hundreds of fish. Without Jesus, we are men most miserable. Without Christ, we are lost in our sins and condemned. Without God's only Son, we have been found guilty and are on our way to hell.

Without Jesus Christ, you can forget about being born-again, changed, or delivered. Without Jesus Christ, mission work ceases, hospitals close, and feeding programs dry up. Without Jesus, you have no hope in the world. There would be no "Away in the Manger," no "Silent Night," no songs like "Noel" or "Joy to the World." Without Jesus, there is no Christmas and no "Come all ye Faithful." Without Jesus, there are no Christmas lights and no giving to others. Without Christ, the lights of the world turn off, because Jesus is the only light. Without Christ, the darkness of the devil controls the hearts of men and women.

Yes friend, <u>Without Jesus Christ</u>, there is no song like "Up From the Grave He Arose." Don Francisco can't sing "He's Alive," and the great hymn of the church, "Amazing Grace" means absolutely nothing.

<u>Without Christ</u>, we can't sing, "Great Is Thy Faithfulness" or "Friendship With Jesus." <u>Without Jesus</u> and His resurrection, we are nothing, we have nothing, and will never be anything. Our heart is empty; our brains become null and void. <u>Without Jesus</u>, we have no abundant life, and no reason for being in existence. <u>Without Christ</u>, there is no rapture, no second coming, and no heaven. <u>Without Jesus</u>, we have no mansion in heaven or streets of gold. <u>Without Christ</u>, there are no crowns, no rewards, and no city without pain. <u>Without Jesus</u>, we have no example of perfect beauty or love. <u>Without Christ</u> and his resurrection, we are dead.

Yes friend, <u>without Jesus Christ</u>, we have no hope, no God and no promise in this life. <u>Without Christ</u>, we have no Bible, for He is the word of God. <u>Without Jesus</u>, we would have no mountains, no rivers, no lakes, no meadows, and no scenery. As a matter of fact, <u>without Christ</u>, we have no physical world. Since Jesus Christ created all tings visible and invisible, <u>without Him</u>, we cease to exist. Only in Christ are we alive and connected to God.

The apostle Paul wrote in 1 Corinthians 15:19, "If in this life only we have hope in Christ, we are of all men most miserable."

First Corinthians 15:20, "But now is Christ risen from the dead, and become the firstfruits of them that slept."

First Corinthians 15:21, "For since by man came death, by man came also the resurrection of the dead."

First Corinthians 15:22, "For as in Adam all die, even so in Christ shall all be made alive."

First Corinthians 15:23, "But every man in his own order: Christ the firstfruits; afterward they that are Christ's at his coming."

First Corinthians 15:24, "Then cometh the end, when he shall have delivered up the kingdom to God, even the Father;

when he shall have put down all rule and all authority and power."

First Corinthians 15:25, "For He must reign, till he hath put all enemies under his feet."

First Corinthians 15:26, "The last enemy that shall be destroyed is death."

First Corinthians 15:27, "For He hath put all things under His feet. But when He saith all things are put under Him, it is manifest that He is excepted, which did put all things under Him."

First Corinthians 15:28, "And when all things shall be subdued unto Him, then shall the Son also Himself be subject unto Him, that God may be all in all."

On this subject, James Denney made this summation: "To put the matter at its simplest, Jesus Christ came to make bad men good."

Origen added, "Although Christ was God, He took flesh; and having been made man, He remained what He was, God."

Martin Luther further explained, "Anything that one imagines of God apart from Christ is only useless thinking and vain idolatry."

World Evangelist Luis Palau remarked, "Jesus Christ's claim of divinity is the most serious claim anyone ever made. Everything about Christianity hinges on His incarnation, crucifixion, and resurrection. That's what Christmas, Good Friday and Easter are all about."

Cyril of Alexandria ties it all together with this quote: "In the person of Christ, a man has not become God; God has become man."

Again the apostle Paul lays out beautifully that Jesus Christ is the only hope of the world. It reads in 1 Corinthians 15:51, "Behold, I shew you a mystery; we shall not all sleep, but we shall all be changed.

First Corinthians 15:52, "In a moment, in the twinkling of an eye, at the last trump: for the trumpet shall sound, and the dead shall be raised incorruptible, and we shall be changed."

First Corinthians 15:53, "For this corruptible must put on incorruption, and this mortal must put on immortality."

First Corinthians 15:54, "So when this corruptible shall have put on incorruption, and this mortal shall have put on immortality, then shall be brought to pass the saying that is written, death is swallowed up in victory."

First Corinthians 15:55, "O death, where is thy sting? O grave, where is thy victory?"

First Corinthians 15:56, "The sting of death is sin; and the strength of sin is the law."

First Corinthians 15:57, "But thanks be to God, which giveth us the victory through our Lord Jesus Christ."

Yes friend, the Victory is through our Lord Jesus Christ. John 3:15 teaches, "That whosoever believeth in Him should not perish, but have eternal life."

John 3:16, "For God so loved the world, that He gave His only begotten Son, that whosoever believeth in Him should not perish but have everlasting life."

John 3:17, "For God sent not his Son into the world to condemn the world; but that the world through Him might be saved."

John 3:18, "He that believeth on Him is not condemned: but he that believeth not is condemned already, because he hath not believed in the name of the only begotten Son of God."

John 3:19, "And this is the condemnation, that light is come unto the world, and men loved darkness rather than light, because their deeds were evil."

Ladies and gentlemen, we serve only one God. God the Father, God the Son, and God the Holy Spirit. Three functions, but only one God. Our entire universe is triune. We are triune and our God is triune.

SEVEN

Answers to Some Tough Questions

It has been my privilege to meet people from many countries of the world. I have met thousands of wonderful sincere people from various religious beliefs. As a result of such extensive travel and social exchange, I deemed it important to answer many of my friends' most earnest questions.

As a human family, we are hoping for peace, health, good families, and prosperity. More so than these is the universal cry for peace of mind and genuine love. However, most of my friends around the world (whether educated or not), agree that to discover the answers to these essential questions, we must first answer the greatest question of all: is there any such thing as absolute truth?

Our generation has produced the philosophy of situational ethics. This doctrine teaches that life is an accident, a mere product of evolution, that there is no God, or if there is one, he lost control or at least he is uninterested in human affairs. It teaches that there are no absolutes.

Situational ethics have given us world conditions and universal transactions without ethics. Human rights have become human wrongs. Human dignity has been swept aside. Scientific pursuit has made peace obsolete. The computer age says that there is nothing totally right or totally wrong. As a result, confusion parades itself to the destruction of the human race. Freedom is not to be found.

Today, situational ethics have given us alcoholism, drug addiction, pornography, homosexuality, infidelity, and greed.

Hundreds of wars are being fought right now, and already millions are suffering from unjust causes.

We live in a selfish society that cries for instant gratification. Sex is taught without standards. As a result, sexually transmitted diseases are at an all time high, while morality struggles are at an all time low. AIDS is killing hundreds of thousands, and newborn babies bear the pain of their parents' sexual impurity. Homes are divided as divorce saturates our world. Freedom is the popular byword, but millions are enslaved.

The youth of the sixties cried for liberty to take drugs and have sex without religious taboos. Many of the same people are imprisoned today by those very things. Today they would rather die. Suicide, as a result, is the final death cry of a world that has gone mad.

Getting in on this act of "anything goes" is modern-day religion. Extrasensory perception (ESP), mind control, and thousands of other mental religions speak of the higher power or knowledge, yet once again without moral standards.

These modern-day religions, like the philosophy of situational ethics, promise freedom but continue to participate in and even help generate the death of the human family. The apostle Peter described it well in 2 Peter, "While they promise them liberty, they themselves are the servants of corruption: for of whom a man is overcome, of the same is he brought in bondage" (2:19).

Situational ethics have given the world despair. They either say that there is no God, or if they admit one exists, they cannot define their god. They claim somewhere in the outer hemisphere is a power where one can receive enlightenment. Yet that power has not changed them for the better or helped society. All these new philosophies and religions are the engineers behind the destruction of our societies. Their creeds and teachings have given us a world filled with violence, hate, and confusion. The world has become a lonely place. People everywhere are in a hurry going nowhere. Left in the shuffle are millions of people who really want the truth.

Unfortunately, many well-known religions have also been affected by situational ethics. The World Council of Churches often times abides by liberation theology. The word "liberation" sounds good, but in reality it promotes atheism and communism. It seems strange that a religious body would help promote its own destruction. Yet, the World Council of Churches seems to be doing just that. They admit that attendance in their mainline churches has dropped to embarrassing lows. By replacing Christianity with religious form and bigotry, these clergy stopped following the Bible and Jesus. Now, each year we see thousands of their followers disenchanted, lonely, and confused. Reality has slipped away, and politics has taken its place. Mans' attempt to please man and pacify the flesh has left God out of the picture. Genuine freedom is lost.

Although most of the world has gone morally mad without regard to conscience, there are still a few religions that have a moral code.

The group that teaches this moral and clean living is doubtlessly the fastest growing religious body in the world. They are called born-again people, or evangelicals, and many times they are referred to as charismatics.

These Christians believe in the literal interpretation of the Bible and have personally experienced the forgiveness and power of Jesus Christ. They claim to have the number one deterrent to drug addiction and alcoholism in the world. An offshoot of this group called Teen Challenge has the number one cure record of drug addicts in America. Their answer is to get each addict to accept Jesus Christ into their lives, which is the born-again experience in John 3:3, and then pray and disciple them in the Bible. The results have been astounding.

In America alone, over 120 million people claim to be born again. Of that number, millions testify of instant deliverance from drugs, alcohol, sexual sins, and diseases when they were converted. More important, every born-again believer testifies of a peace that passes human understanding. They all testify of a newfound love and joy. Born-again people testify of a changed life when Christ forgives them of their sins.

Most of the born-again people, although there are some exceptions, leave denominational churches and join independent Bible churches. These independent churches are the largest and fastest growing. Dr. Cho's church in Seoul, South Korea is a prime example. It is charismatic and is the largest church in the world. His church has over 1 million members and will, with a few other groups, have 100 percent of the South Korean people born again by the year 2005.

There are many other charismatic churches in the world that have tens of thousands in their congregations. Their services are alive and very exciting. They pray for the sick, and therefore, experiencing genuine miracles is the norm, not the exception. Many call them the happiest people on the earth. To these "Jesus-people," God is loving and forgiving. Though they believe judgment day is coming, they emphasize the grace of Christ, which is taught in the New Testament. Around the world, millions are being born again every year. Africa alone boasts of eleven thousand new born-again converts per day. Thousands of Catholics, Muslims, Hindus, and Buddhists are coming to Christ and getting their lives changed.

Besides their emphasis on a personal experience with their loving God, born-again Christians are the world leaders in feeding the poor, clothing the naked, and giving shelter to the homeless. Tens of thousands of charismatic and evangelical groups help millions of hurting people each year throughout the world. They do it because they love people and want to please Christ.

Though there have been a few well-documented moral failures (such as the television evangelists in the late 1980s), most of these born-again Christians live consistent moral and godly lives. Jesus called them the salt of the earth and the light of the world.

I am grateful to be a part of this group, but most of all to have experienced the forgiveness of Jesus Christ. Jesus has personally answered my prayers on thousands of occasions. I've seen hundreds of miracles of divine origin. My own father was healed of an incurable disease, and Jesus healed my barren wife; today we have three beautiful children.

Though born-again Christians have done so much for society, they are without a doubt the most persecuted religious group in the world. Christian bashing seems to be the media's top priority. Simply put, the reason is conviction. People who aren't born again get under conviction about their own sin. Instead of turning to Christ, they ridicule the Christians. They think attacking us or trying to somehow discredit us gets them off the hook. But, of course, it doesn't! Someday, all will stand before Jesus Christ at the Great White Throne of Judgment.

The Hebrew writer wrote, "It is appointed unto men once to die and after this the judgment," And John the Revelator wrote, "And I saw the dead, small and great, stand before God; and the books were opened: and another book was opened, which is the book of life: and the dead were judged out of those things which were written in the books, according to their works" (Revelation 20:12).

Jesus Himself, said in Mark 16:15, "And he said unto them, 'Go ye into all the world, and preach the gospel to every creature'." Mark 16:16, "He that believeth and is baptized shall be saved; but he that believeth not shall be damned." Jesus wasn't crucified because of His incredible miracle-working power. He was crucified because of what He said. Jesus spoke out against sin and then confessed to be God. Jesus irritated two thousand years of new religions when he said in John 14:6, "Jesus saith unto him, I am the Way, the Truth, and the Life: no man cometh unto the Father but by me." Such a narrow belief system is too much for people who love darkness more than light. So, as a born-again believer in Christ, I gladly accept persecution, even death for my Lord and Savior. Jesus said that the gospel is an offense to those who refuse to listen. As God's Word says, "The bond woman will always try to kill the free woman." Simply put, those in darkness resent those in light, especially when the light shines upon their darkness of sin and unbelief.

So we rejoice when we are persecuted for righteousness sake.

Matthew 5:10, "Blessed are they which are persecuted for righteousness' sake: for theirs is the kingdom of heaven."

Matthew 5:11, "Blessed are ye, when men shall revile you, and persecute you, and shall say all manner of evil against you falsely, for my sake."

Matthew 5:12, "Rejoice, and be exceedingly glad: for great is your reward in heaven: for so persecuted they the prophets which were before you."

If the persecution comes from other religions or even from hypocritical Christian ranks (those who deny the faith they confess), we rejoice for we are no better than our Savior. As Paul the apostle wrote in, Philippians 3:10, "That I may know him, and the power of his resurrection, and the fellowship of his sufferings, being made comfortable unto his death;"

According to the Bible, you can't be a Christian unless you're born again. In John 3:3, "Jesus answered and said unto him, Verily, verily, I say unto thee, except a man be born again, he cannot see the kingdom of God."

He went on in verses 5-8 and explained, "Verily, verily, I say unto thee, Except a man be born of water and of the Spirit, he cannot enter into the kingdom of God. That which is born of the flesh is flesh; and that which is born of the Spirit is spirit. Marvel not that I said unto thee, Ye must be born again. The wind bloweth where it listeth, and thou hearest the sound thereof, but canst not tell whence it cometh, and whither it goeth: so is every one that is born of the Spirit."

Jesus is saying that you can't see the wind itself, only the evidence of it. No man can see the Spirit of God enter a person, but we can see the evidence of such a phenomenon. I have never seen God's Holy Spirit go into a convert. But I have witnessed the changed life that has resulted.

People who are born again experience a new life. The apostle Paul wrote in 2 Corinthians 5:17, "Therefore if any man be in Christ, he is a new creature: old things are passed away; behold all things are become new."

This born-again experience is when Christ comes into our lives by the Holy Spirit. Paul wrote, "I live, yet not I, but Christ liveth in me" (Galatians 2:20). The apostle John said, "Greater is He that is in me than he that is in the world" (see 1 John 4:4).

The Bible teaches that a person who is born again has the Spirit of God living in him. The apostle Paul wrote in 2 Corinthians 3:16-17, "Know ye not that ye are the temple of God, and that the Spirit of God dwelleth in you? If any man defile the temple of God, him shall God destroy; for the temple of God is holy, which temple ye are."

First Corinthians 2:12, "Now we have received, not the spirit of the world, but the Spirit which is of God."

Jesus himself said in Revelation 3:20, "Behold, I stand at the door and knock: if any man hear my voice, and open the door, I will come in to him, and will sup with him, and he with me."

There are millions of people worldwide who claim to be Christians, but have never experienced Jesus personally. These people try by outward works to live Christian lives, but fail miserably; Christ doesn't live there. They have profession without possession.

As a matter of fact, there are entire Christian denominations that even deny the born-again experience, plus other supernatural experiences in Scripture. Years ago, this wasn't the case. Sin has not only crept into politics, but religion as well. Entire denominations have left their original faith in Christ and have taken on situational ethics. No wonder millions of people in these denominations leave their churches every year and join independent Bible believing churches.

Millions of people today want the reality of Christ, not a bunch of hypocritical religious practices. That is one of the many reasons the born-again experience is sweeping the world. Yet, the number one reason is the reality of Christ in a person's life and the guarantee of eternal life in Heaven.

Jesus Christ in the Bible

Old Testament:
- In Genesis He is the seed of the woman
- In Exodus the Lamb for sinners slain
- In Leviticus our High Priest
- In Numbers the star of Jacob

- In Deuteronomy the Prophet like unto Moses and the Great Rock
- In Joshua the captain of the Lord of Hosts
- In Judges the Messenger of Jehovah
- In Ruth our Kinsman-Redeemer and faithful Bridegroom
- In 1 Samuel He is seen as the Great Judge
- In 2 Samuel He is the Princely King
- In 1 Kings, as David's choice
- In 2 Kings, as the Holiest of all
- In 1 Chronicles, as the King by birth
- In 2 Chronicles, as King by judgment
- In Ezra, He is seen as Lord of heaven and earth
- In Nehemiah, as the Builder
- In Esther, our Mordecai
- In Job, our Daysman and our risen returning Redeemer
- In Psalms, the Son of God and the Good Shepherd
- In Proverbs, our Wisdom
- In Ecclesiastes, as the One above the sun
- In the Song of Solomon, the great church lover, the One altogether lovely, and the Chiefest among ten thousand
- In Isaiah, He is the suffering and Glorified Servant
- In Jeremiah, the Lord, our righteousness
- In Lamentations, the Man of sorrows
- In Ezekiel, the Glorious God
- In Daniel, the Smithing Stone and the Messiah
- In Hosea, He is the Risen Son of God
- In Joel, the Out-pourer of the Spirit
- In Amos, the Eternal Christ
- In Obadiah, the Forgiving Christ
- In Micah, the Bethlehemite
- In Nahum, He is the Bringer of Good Tidings
- In Habakkuk, the Lord in His Holy Temple
- In Zephaniah, the Merciful Christ
- In Haggai, the Desire of All Nations
- In Zechariah, the Branch
- In Malachi, the Son of Righteousness with healing in his wings

New Testament:

- In Matthew, He is the King of the Jews
- In Mark, the Servant
- In Luke, the perfect Son of Man
- In John, the Son of God
- In Acts, He is the Ascended Lord
- In Romans, the Lord our righteousness
- In 1 Corinthians, our resurrection
- In 2 Corinthians, our Comforter
- In Galatians, the End of the Law
- In Ephesians, the Head of the Church
- In Philippians, the Supplier of every need
- In Colossians, the Fullness of the Godhead
- In 1 Thessalonians, He comes for his Church
- In 2 Thessalonians, He comes with his Church
- In 1 Timothy, He is the Mediator
- In 2 Timothy, the Bestower of Crowns
- In Titus, our Great God and Savior
- In Philemon, the Prayer of Crowns
- In Hebrews, the Rest of the Faith and Fulfiller of Types
- In James, the Lord Drawing High
- In 1 Peter, the Vicarious Sufferer
- In 2 Peter, the Lord of Glory
- In 1 John, the Way
- In 2 John, the Truth
- In 3 John, the Life
- In Jude, He is our Security
- In Revelation, the Lion of the Tribe of Judah, the Lamb of
- God, the Bright and Morning Star, the Kings of Kings, and the Lord of Lords.

EIGHT

Destination Heaven

Revelation 21:4, "And God shall wipe away all tears from their eyes; and there shall be no more death, neither sorrow, nor crying, neither shall there be any more pain: for the former things are passed away."

As a small boy being raised in a Pentecostal church, I can remember the excitement of that Hermiston, Oregon congregation when they sang "Looking for a City." The joy that filled those people was remarkable and had a profound impact on my life. There was no doubt they believed what they were singing. Even though I was only about five years old, I too believed. Today, however, I believe even more that there is a literal of bliss called Heaven. It's everything people hope for, plus a lot more.

First Corinthians 2:9, "But as it is written, eye hath not seen, nor ear heard, neither have entered into the heart of man, the things which God hath prepared for them that love Him."

The Bible says we should believe in heaven as strongly as the Old Testament believers. The Bible says the Old Testament believers declared plainly that they sought a country whose foundation builder was God. It says they were persuaded of their eternal life and that they embraced its total reality. They confessed they were but strangers and pilgrims in this life on a journey to the Promised Land. Even Moses chose to suffer affliction with the people of God, rather than to enjoy the pleasures of sin for a season (Hebrews 11:25).

Hebrews 11:26, "Esteeming the reproach of Christ greater riches than the treasures in Egypt: for he had respect unto the recompence of the reward."

Hebrews 13:14, "For here have we no continuing city, but we seek one to come."

First Peter 1:4, "To an inheritance incorruptible, and undefiled, and that fadeth not away, reserved in heaven for you."

This wonderful place called heaven is given other various names to describe its purpose and beauty. Heaven is also referred to as Mount Zion.

Hebrews 12:22, "But ye are come unto mount Sion, and unto the city of the living God, the heavenly Jerusalem, and to an innumerable company of angels,"

Psalm 48:1, "Great is the Lord, and greatly to be praised in the city of our God, in the mountain of His holiness."

Zechariah 6:1, "And I turned, and lifted up mine eyes, and looked, and, behold, there came four chariots out from between two mountains; and the mountains were mountains of brass."

Most descriptions of heaven are of the holy city called the New Jerusalem. It is so beautiful our minds won't fully comprehend it, until we see it in person. However, God does give us some idea regarding various attributes of heaven: its dimensions and how it operates. It is very clear that God wants us to "get our hopes up" and look forward to such a wonderful place; a genuine paradise with no disappointments.

God Is in Heaven

John 14:1, "Let not your heart be troubled: ye believe in God, believe also in me."

John 14:2, "In my Father's house are many mansions: if it were not so, I would have told you. I go to prepare a place for you."

John 14:3, "And if I go and prepare a place for you, I will come again, and receive you unto myself; that where I am, there ye may be also."

Heaven is an incredible place, (first of all) because God lives there. Scriptures plainly teach we shall see Christ face to face and have eternal fellowship with God.

Revelation 21:3, "And I heard a great voice out of heaven saying, Behold, the tabernacle of God is with men, and will dwell with them, and they shall be his people, and God himself shall be with them, and be their God."

Revelation 21:6, "And he said unto me, It is done. I am Alpha and Omega, the beginning and the end. I will give unto him that is athirst of the fountain of the water of life freely."

Revelation 21:7, "He that overcometh shall inherit all things; and I will be his God, and he shall be my son."

Heaven is a place where we will worship God, work for God, and be blessed by God for eternity. It will be a happy-forever family reunion with our creator.

Revelation 5:9, "And they sung a new song, saying, Thou art worthy to take the book, and to open the seals thereof: for thou wast slain, and hast redeemed us to God by the blood out of every kindred and tongue, and people, and nation;"

Revelation 7:15, "Therefore are they before the throne of God, and serve him day and night in His temple: and He sitteth on the throne shall dwell among them."

Revelation 7:16, "They shall hunger no more, neither thirst any more; neither shall the sun light on them, nor any heat."

Revelation 7:17, "For the Lamb which is in the midst of the throne shall feed them, and shall lead them unto living fountains of waters: and God shall wipe away all tears from their eyes."

The prophet Isaiah must have seen similar quality of heaven and of God when he wrote, "They shall not hunger nor thirst; neither shall the heat nor sun smite them: for He that hath mercy on them shall lead them, even by the springs of water shall He guide them" (49:10).

First Peter 3:22, "Who is gone into heaven, and is on the right hand of God; angels and authorities and powers being made subject to him."

Ephesians 4:10, "He that descended is the same also that ascended up far above all heavens, that He might fill all things."

John 14:13, "And whatsoever ye shall ask in my name, that will I do, that the Father may be glorified in the Son."

Ephesians 2:18, "For through him we both have access by one Spirit unto the Father."

Second Corinthians 5:1, "For we know that if our earthly house of this tabernacle were dissolved, we have a building of God, an house not made with hands, eternal in the heavens."

John the apostle also confirmed the fact that we shall see God.

First John 2:3, "And hereby we do know that we know Him, if we keep his commandments."

What a joy it is to think someday we will see God and be with Christ forever. Some of us may experience our Lord's second coming or the rapture, and others may die first. But the fact is that when we see Him, everything wonderful will take place. The songwriter had it right: "Oh, I want to see Him, look upon His face. There to sing forever of His saving grace. On the streets of glory let me lift my voice. Cares all past, home at last, ever to rejoice."

Description of Heaven

Besides the fact that heaven is a place of peace, it is also a city of beauty. In chapter 21 of Revelation, we get a very clear description of the Holy City.

Mount Zion is fifteen hundred miles square (twelve thousand furlongs) with the holy temple being at the very northern peak. Descending down from the holy temple are twelve broadways which are transparent gold (looks like transparent glass). Each of these twelve broadways has a river flowing in it midst, and on each side of the rivers are trees of life. The leaves on the trees give the life needed for humans to maintain extended health. These broadways and rivers descend from the holy temple (fifteen hundred miles high) down through twelve gates (the gates are large pearls) and out into the newly created earth (after the second coming of Christ) to bring healing to the nations.

Revelation 22:1, "And he shewed me a pure river of water of life, clear as crystal, proceeding out of the throne of God and of the Lamb."

Revelation 22:2, "In the midst of the street of it, and on either side of the river, was there the tree of life, which bare twelve manner of fruits, and yielded her fruit every month: and the leaves of the tree were for the healing of the nations."

Revelation 21:18, "And the building of the wall of it was of jasper: and the city was pure gold, like unto clear glass."

Revelation 21:19, "And the foundations of the wall of the city were garnished with all manner of precious stones. The first foundation was jasper; the second sapphire; the third, a chalcedony; the fourth, an emerald;"

Revelation 21:20, "The fifth, sardonyx; the sixth, sardius; the seventh, chrysolyte; the eighth, beryl; the ninth, a topaz; the tenth, a chrysoprasus; the eleventh, a jacinth; the twelfth, an amethyst."

In case you may be unsure what the various stones look like, the following is a brief description. Jasper has a green sea color; sapphire is a hard, blue stone; chalcedony is a yellow-red (or bluish white) transparent stone; emerald is a green stone; sardonyx is a red agate stone; sardius is a blood red stone; chrysolyte is a gold stone, dusty green with a yellow cast; beryl is a bluish-green transparent gem; topaz is a pale green gem with a mixture of yellow; chrysoprasus is a yellowish-green stone; jacinth is a red, cinnamon color stone; and amethyst is a purple stone composed of strong blue and deep red.

For a moment, try to imagine a city of gold fifteen hundred miles in square diameter, with twelve great boulevards and rivers going into twelve pearl gates. Now imagine all of those twelve boulevards as transparent gold and the rivers each lined with trees of everlasting health. Besides all of this, the Bible tells us of many other lakes and rivers, and our own personal mansions. Add to that all of the personal blessing, no pain, tears, sorrow, etc. and many delights of working for Jesus the King.

To put it simply, heaven is a paradise that the human mind can't even begin to fully understand. However, it is a real place, and your eternal choice is either heaven or hell.

The People Who Go to Heaven

Heaven is made up of people who have been born-again by the Spirit of God. This "born-again" experience takes place when people humble themselves, repent of their sins, and invite Jesus Christ into their life. At that precious moment, Jesus, by his shed blood on Calvary washes their sins, away and then comes into their life by His Holy Spirit.

Second Corinthians 5:17, "Therefore if any man be in Christ, he is a new creature: old things are passed away; behold all things are become new."

Second Corinthians 5:18, "And all things are of God, Who hath reconciled us to Himself by Jesus Christ, and hath given to us the ministry of reconciliation;"

This born-again experience, (John 3:3), is essential for entrance into heaven. The Bible teaches that when you are born again, (also ascribed to as saved, redeemed, reconciled), your name is instantly written in the Lamb's Book of Life.

Revelation 21:22, "And I saw no temple therein: for the Lord God Almighty and the Lamb are the temple of it."

Jesus sent the seventy out to preach the gospel, heal the sick, and cast out devils (Luke 10). When they returned, the seventy were rejoicing over the fact that the devils were subject to them. Our Lord's reply to them shows us the importance of being born again.

Luke 10:19, "Behold, I give unto you power to tread on serpents and scorpions, and over all the power of the enemy: and nothing shall by any means hurt you."

Luke 10:20, "Notwithstanding in this rejoice not, that the spirits are subject unto you; but rather rejoice, because your names are written in Heaven."

Jesus was speaking on the subject of priorities. What is most important is your salvation. Our Lord stressed the importance of salvation far more than any other subject. If your name is written in the Lamb's Book of Life, you get to go to heaven; if it isn't, you will spend eternity in hell.

Revelation 20:15, "And whosoever was not found written in the book of life was cast into the lake of fire."

Saved by Grace to Win the Race!

We are saved by God's grace, not of works, lest anyone should boast. This is the foundation of the gospel (good news) message. NO one in their own righteousness deserves heaven, but while we were yet sinners, Christ died for us. However, as Paul made it clear, we are not saved by grace to live on in sin. We are saved by grace, empowered by the Holy Spirit to finish what we started. We are exhorted in Scripture to run our race to win (Hebrews 12:1).

However, even when we finish the race, we will not be able to say that we saved ourselves. Only by God's grace can we have enough strength to finish the race. For we are saved by grace and sustained by faith.

The people in heaven are people who trusted Jesus to sustain them through all experiences, sins, and temptations of life. They learned how to lean on Jesus through every storm and drew from His power to conquer every battle. They are not perfect people, but were smart enough to know they couldn't save themselves (and when you realize you can't save yourself, Jesus is ready to save you; at that point, you come to understand what grace is all about).

You can try to be a good person for the next hundred years, and you will split hell wide open. The Bible makes it clear: there's only one Savior, one Answer, one Mediator, one Way, and only one faith, the Lord Jesus Christ. Jesus is your only chance. Without Him, you have no hope of even making it into the kingdom of heaven.

Last Day Mockers

There will be, in the last day, mockers and grace-blasphemers who will tempt God, and because of constant sin, will drop out of the race and actually serve Satan. These people, who once knew Christ, will backslide, lose their salvation, and burn in hell for eternity.

It's sad to see so many in the condition of spiritual depravity. They once knew God's love and grace, but they left the race, fell in love with the world, and today mock God by their own sinful lusts. The Bible makes it clear; these people, unless they repent will not inherit the kingdom of God.

The people who go to heaven are people who know Jesus Christ in a personal way. Many people know Christ in a historical way, or a religious way, but they don't know Jesus in a personal way.

When you repent of your sins, renounce your old sinful nature, believe on Jesus, and confess Him as Lord, you are born-again. At that precise moment, you personally are introduced to Jesus Christ, and His Holy Spirit comes into your life. From that moment on you grow in grace and in the image of Jesus Christ.

At the point of conversion, you can take the promise of Jesus Himself that He will never leave you nor forsake you, and no man can take you out of His hands. You can have assurance of eternal security as long as you keep walking with Christ and repenting when you fall. As long as you are sincere, Jesus will forgive you at least 490 times a day (seventy times seven). As long as you try, Jesus will never say good-bye. Jesus will never leave you, and no man can ever take your salvation. However, if you keep living in sin, refuse to repent, and eventually lose faith in God, you, by your own rebellion, can walk away from Christ. Of course, backsliding is a pain, because the devil will taunt you, and God's spirit will convict you. It's far better to stay in the race and finish it, and receive the crown of life in heaven.

However, if you have backslidden, come home to Jesus right now. Turn to Jesus with all your heart, and like the prodigal son, you will be forgiven and received back into the Kingdom of God.

The world has nothing to offer that can match the promises of God. Jesus said, "For what is a man profited, if he shall gain the whole world, and lose his own soul?" (Matthew 16:26). Christ made it clear, "The flesh profits nothing; it is the Spirit that quickens."

Philippians 4:8, "Finally brethren, whatsoever things are true, whatsoever things are honest, whatsoever things are just, whatsoever things are pure, whatsoever things are lovely, whatsoever things are of good report; if there be and virtue, and if there be any praise, think on these things."

Galatians 2:16, "Knowing that a man is not justified by the works of the law, but by the faith of Jesus Christ, even we have believed in Jesus Christ, that we might be justified by the faith of Christ, and not by the works of the law: for by the works of the law shall no flesh be justified."

You can be saved right now by simply putting your faith and trust in the Lord Jesus Christ. You can have eternal life right now by repenting of your sin and asking Christ into your heart. You will be changed instantly. The moment you call upon the name of the Lord, you will know Christ personally and be assured of everlasting life in Heaven. Yes, Heaven is a beautiful place where we are invited to live with Jesus for eternity.

Revelation 22:14, "Blessed are they that do His commandments, that they may have right to the tree of life, and may enter in through the gates into the city."

Revelation 22:15, "For without are dogs, and sorcerers, and whoremongers, and murderers, and idolaters, and whosoever loveth and maketh a lie."

Revelation 22:17, "And the Spirit and the bride say, 'Come.' And let him that heareth say, 'Come.' And let him that is athirst come. And whosoever will, let him take the water of life freely."

The Love and Judgment of God

Throughout the Bible, we see the love and judgment of God in action. Both His love and judgment are inseparable. Like two sides of a coin, you must recognize God's love and judgment as one.

God shows and offers you His love through His Son, the Lord Jesus Christ. However, if you reject Jesus, you will be introduced to His fiery judgment.

The judgment of God encompasses two basic human errors. The first error is the sin of rebellion. Whenever you break a commandment of God (lust, adultery, lying, etc...) you are in rebellion. The second error is the sin of lukewarmness, or apathy.

Revelation 3:15, "I know thy works, that thou art neither cold nor hot: I would thou wert cold or hot."

Revelation 3:16, "So then because thou art lukewarm, and neither cold or hot, I will spue thee out of my mouth."

There are many of you who you don't consider yourselves hard-ridden sinners, but you're in a tragic situation. Your lukewarmness will send you to hell.

One man asked the question, "What's worse, ignorance or apathy?" The other answered, "I don't know and I don't care."

We live in a generation of wealth and prosperity. As a result, many millions of people see no need for a god. Their complacency and lethargy are keeping them from true wealth.

Revelation 3:17, "Because thou sayest, I am rich, and increased with goods, and have need of nothing; and knowest not that thou art wretched, and miserable, and poor, and blind, and naked:"

Revelation 3:19, "As many as I love, I rebuke and chasten: be zealous therefore, and repent."

Revelation 3:20, "Behold, I stand at the door, and knock: if any man hear my voice, and open the door, I will come in to him, and will sup with him, and he with me."

Revelation 3:21, "To him that overcometh will I grant to sit with me in my throne, even as I also overcame, and am set down with my Father in His throne."

Payday Someday

Dr. C. M. Ward (worldwide radio evangelist and author) tells of the time he arrived in Dallas for a convention. The hotel staff greeted him with a tremendous welcome. Flowers and fruits of various kinds were found in his room and a personal welcome came from the management.

As a matter of fact, when he first went to the lobby desk, the manager asked, "Are you THE C. M. Ward?" Upon learning that he was THE C. M. Ward in the flesh, the manger went out of his way to make Dr. Ward feel comfortable.

The manager told Dr. Ward to help himself to their many restaurants, shops, and services. Everything was taken care of as Dr. Ward lived it up like a king. He ate three great meals daily, used all their in-house services and bought many nice gifts in their shops. Dr. Ward thoroughly lived it up for a solid week. He could hardly believe the respect and generosity of his hosts.

When it came time to check out, C. M. just signed his name and left with such a great feeling. It was a tremendous week of living like a true celebrity. Everything was paid for and he just signed his name. After getting home, Rev. Ward told his lovely wife Dorothy all about his wonderful experience in Dallas. He said, "Dorothy, I wish you could have enjoyed it with me."

After visiting for a while with his wife and telling her all about his first-class treatment, Dorothy quietly showed him a very large bill from a prominent hotel in Dallas, Texas. You guessed it, the nice place kept a record of meals and expenses and billed Dr. Ward in full. What Dr. Ward thought was a free ride turned out to be a "pay-in-full."

Luckily for Dr. Ward, he had money in the reserve for such a payday. He and Dorothy had been saving money all along and as a result were prepared for such a great judgment.

Dr. Ward's lesson will be realized by millions of people in the judgment day, but they will not be so prepared.

Many of you will also be in that crowd. You have been breathing God's air, drinking His water, eating His food, enjoying His sunshine, and spending time in His lakes. You've been enjoying God's mountains and oceans and have thoroughly used God's resources in the earth. You may think you have no need of God, but you have been using all of God's creation. Payday is coming.

When you get to heaven, God is going to ask you to pay in full. Some of you will say, "Well, Lord, I have a boat and a motor home back home in the garage that I'll give you. And I'll even give you my home and all my savings."

But God, you see, isn't impressed with our things. The Bible says Heaven's streets are pure gold, and that God owns the cattle on a thousand hills. So the Lord will say "Insufficient funds."

Since you will be unable to pay off your debt, someone else must pay your ransom. That person is the Lord Jesus Christ. Jesus is your life insurance, where the premium has already been paid. Of course, to know that your debt is paid in full, you must know Christ personally. That's why it's so important to not be complacent about the things of God. That's why it's so important to live for Jesus Christ each day of your life and always be ready to face God. That's why you must be born again.

The people who go to heaven are people who are living their lives for Jesus Christ. These are the ones who have experienced God's grace to finish the race.

Invitation

Revelation 3:20, "Behold, I stand at the door, and knock: if any man hear my voice, and open the door, I will come in to him, and will sup with him, and he with me."

Jesus is standing at your heart's door knocking. He is asking permission to come into your life, have daily fellowship with you, and give you eternal life in Heaven.

Jesus said, "If any man hear my voice and open the door, I will come in." The simplicity is clear; all you must do is hear His voice and open the door. The Lord Jesus will do the rest.

Throughout your life, Jesus has been knocking at your door. Many of you have tried to ignore it, run from it, and even at times curse it. But the knock is still there, and you must forever make a decision for Christ.

I believe that even during the reading of this book, you have heard God's voice. Just by reading the many Bible verses, you are hearing from God.

Now, it's probably not an audible voice, but it is an inner tugging in your spirit. On one hand, you feel drawn toward God and on the other you feel rebellious. This is normal, and all sinners go through that struggle before surrendering to Jesus Christ.

Since you have already heard God's voice, now all you must do is open the door of your heart and invite Jesus Christ into your life.

Now, some of you may ask, "Why would I want to let Christ into my life?" The answer is simple: sin is an incurable disease that will eventually kill you physically, emotionally, and spiritually, and will forever put you in a lake of fire. Once you realize the tragedy of sin and realize that Jesus Christ is the only escape, you will quickly open your heart to Jesus.

You May Be a Good Person

You may be a very good person. Perhaps you are a faithful husband, a good mother, an honest person, and you say, "I'm better than most Christians."

As I mentioned earlier in this book and as the Bible plainly teaches, "All have sinned." The Bible says, "Our righteousness is as filthy rags to God" (see Isaiah 64:6). No person will ever get into heaven by just being good. Our goodness is filthy rags to God. You're only made good enough by the blood of Jesus. That is why you must open your heart in repentance and invite Christ into your life. At that point, you are instantly and gloriously born again. The Bible tells the story of a general called Naaman in the Syrian army who was a great man, a mighty man in valor, and was considered honorable. The Lord God had used Naaman to bring deliverance unto Syria (2 Kings 5:1).

Even though Naaman was such a great and respected man, he had one major problem: he was a leper.

Now, leprosy was considered a type of sin. It was distasteful, incurable, and physically handicapping. No matter what great plaque or trophy Naaman had received, it was all for naught. He had to get rid of his leprosy.

Sir, ma'am, you are just like Naaman. Your sin is not leprosy, but pride, and unless you get rid of it and invite Christ to wash you clean, all your accomplishments are worth nothing. Jesus warned us, if we gain the whole world, but lost our own soul, we've gained nothing, but lost everything.

If you had an incurable physical disease like Naaman, I'm sure you would do everything in your power to be cured. For example, millions of dollars are spent each year by people with cancer, AIDS, and other incurable diseases. There is no price tag too high when you are dying. Yet, the most dangerous disease of all is usually overlooked and ignored. It's the disease of sin that will damn your soul for eternity in hell. How much would you give to have eternal life? How much would you give to escape hellfire?

The Bible price is free. Salvation is a free gift, but is only received via genuine humility, repentance, and faith in God.

Ephesians 2:8, "For by grace are ye saved through faith; and that not of yourselves: it is the gift of God:"

Ephesians 2:9, "Not of works, lest any man should boast."

God hates pride and no person will ever stand in heaven and say, "I earned this." Your only way to salvation is by grace, and the only way to experience God's grace is to die to yourself, take up your cross and follow Christ. That means humility.

Proverbs 8:13, "The fear of the Lord is to hate evil: pride, and arrogancy, and the evil way, and the froward mouth, do I hate."

Naaman had to experience humility before he experienced salvation and healing. The Bible tells us that this great general departed and took with him ten talents of silver and six thousand pieces of gold and ten changes of raiment and went on a long journey with his servants to the Lord of Samaria to be healed by a prophet named Elisha.

Second Kings 5:5, "And the king of Syria said, 'Go to, go, and I will send a letter unto the king of Israel.' And he departed, and took with him ten talents of silver, and six thousand pieces of gold, and ten changes of raiment."

The money value taken by Naaman would exceed seventy-seven thousand American dollars. Naaman was planning on paying for his healing. As you can imagine, Naaman was desperate to be free from his leprosy.

How desperate are you to get rid of your sin? How much is your eternal soul worth to you? Are you willing to take the spiritual journey of humility and let Christ come into your life? To do so, you must admit to God that you can't save yourself.

Naaman realized he couldn't save himself. He humbled himself by going to a faith healer, but soon discovered he wasn't humble enough.

Upon arriving at the prophet's house (Elisha, the healer, man of God), Naaman was given what he thought was a cold shoulder. No respect, no courtesy, but almost rudeness was the response.

Second Kings 5:9, "So Naaman came with his horses and with his chariot, and stood at the door of the house of Elisha."

Second Kings 5:10, "And Elisha sent a messenger unto him, saying, Go and wash in Jordan seven times, and thy flesh shall come again to thee, and thou shalt be clean."

Naaman was right about one thing, the rivers of Abana and Pharpar were much more clean than the muddy Jordan. But God wanted to free Naaman from the sin and bondage of pride. God wouldn't allow Elisha to show him respect, nor take his payment for healing, but rather told him to dip in a stinky, smelly, dirty river.

God was not impressed with Naaman's statistics, courage, or honor. God was not impressed with Naaman's money or prestige. God was only concerned about Naaman's soul.

The Lord doesn't want to humble you to torment you. God only wants to humble you to free you.

Proverbs 16:18, "Pride goeth before destruction, and an haughty spirit before a fall."

The Lord wants to keep you from destruction; He wants to keep you from falling. Pride is a form of rebellion that leads to hell. Yes, God wanted to cure Naaman of his leprosy, just like the Lord wants to heal you of various afflictions. But most important to God was Naaman's spiritual condition. The Lord wanted to see Naaman "born of His Spirit," totally converted with all of his sins forgiven. The outward leprosy was just a token of what God intended to do for Naaman's inward man. A sick body can go to Heaven, but never a sick soul.

Even though at first Naaman rejected the prophet's instructions, he later, upon bidding of his servants, gave heed and went down to the muddy Jordan.

Second Kings 5:13, "And his servants came near, and spake unto him and said, My father, if the prophet had bid thee do some great thing, wouldest thou not have done it? How much rather then, when he saith to thee, 'Wash, and be clean'?"

Now their reasoning with Naaman makes sense even today. The three words that stand out in the above verse are "some great thing."

For example, if you say to a person, "To be saved and go to heaven you must go to church each day, give to the poor, quit cussing, join our church, and be a good person," you may have more converts than preaching grace. Yes, if you say to a person, "To be saved you must shave your head and wear a robe," you may get more converts than preaching grace in Jesus.

This is evident around the world. Many millions of people sacrifice their bodies (some Muslims stab themselves) and go through many religious ceremonies to be saved. But if you say to these people, "You must repent, humble yourself, and totally rely on Christ for salvation, they reject it.

There are many cults that way; the way of heaven comes via selling all you have, giving it to the cult founders, and living in a commune. Many are doing this even today. People will pay for salvation with their bodies, their minds, their works, their associations, and with their religious activity. But tell them salvation is by grace alone, and they are instantly offended.

Your number one sin is pride—until you repent of it and humble yourself, you will never know the grace of Jesus Christ.

You see, Naaman's servants were very smart. They reasoned with him and probably said other things such as, "Look, Naaman, you brought over seventy-seven thousand dollars to pay for your healing, you would give that much, why then is dipping seven times in the Jordan so difficult?"

Well, in the physical realm, dipping seven times in a muddy river can be accomplished quickly and easily. But in the social, high-class realm of status, it was a very difficult thing to do. Naaman would have to swallow all his pride in front of his men, give in to a rude prophet, Elisha, and become totally dependent not on his money, but on God alone.

Though it was difficult, Naaman did go to the Jordan and he went down seven times.

Second Kings 5:14, "Then went he down, and dipped himself seven times in Jordan, according to the saying of the man of God: and his flesh came again like unto the flesh of a little child, and he was clean."

Because he finally humbled himself, Naaman received not only a physical healing, but also eternal salvation from God. Naaman must have experienced tremendous joy and relief when he looked upon his own skin and instead of seeing sores, he saw new skin like that of a child.

The words that stand out to me are "and he was clean." Those four words describe salvation. God cleans you up and puts His Holy Spirit in you and washes away every sin and stain. To be clean is to be free. To be free is to be saved. To be saved is to be found in heaven. To be found in heaven is to have known humility and the grace of God.

Don't Offer Olive Branches

When Jesus rode into Jerusalem, the crowds were moved with great emotion and cried.

Matthew 21:8, "And a very great multitude spread their garments in the way; others cut down branches from the trees, and strawed them in the way."

Matthew 21:9, "And the multitudes that went before, and that followed, cried, saying, 'Hosanna to the Son of David: Blessed is He that cometh in the name of the Lord; Hosanna in the highest'."

Offering Jesus things is good when it is accomplished with fresh surrender. But to offer things without repentance is a slap in the face of God.

What God wants from you is a sincere heart that trusts God for total salvation.

Micah 5:6, "And they shall waste the land of Assyria with the sword, and the land of Nimrod in the entrances thereof: thus shall He deliver us from the Assyrian, when He cometh into our land, and when He treadeth within our borders."

Micah 5:7, "And the remnant of Jacob shall be in the midst of many people as a dew from the Lord, as the showers upon the grass, that tarrieth not for man, nor waiteth for the sons of men."

Micah 5:8, "And the remnant of Jacob shall be among the Gentiles in the midst of many people as a lion among the beasts of the forest, as a young lion among the flocks of sheep: who, if he go through, both treadeth down, and teareth in pieces, and none can deliver."

Isaiah 1:18, "Come now, and let us reason together, saith the Lord: though your sins be as scarlet, they shall be as white as snow; though they be red like crimson, they shall be as wool."

Isaiah 1:19, "If ye be willing and obedient, ye shall eat the good of the land."

Isaiah 1:20, "But if ye refuse and rebel, ye shall be devoured with the sword: for the mouth of the Lord hath spoken it."

The Choice Is Yours

Whether you live in heaven or live in hell is determined by your personal decision. No one can decide for you. If you want to continue to serve the devil, you are able to do so. God forces no one into salvation; the Lord only offers Jesus as the door of escape.

Many of you have debated religion and stood by your false viewpoint for so long, you would rather go to hell than have to admit you were wrong. What a sad, eternal tragedy.

However, I am sure there are those of you who have read this book and you now fully understand salvation and you want to be saved. To you I say, "Congratulations, this is the greatest day of your life, and for eternity you will never be sorry."

The choice is yours. You can choose life or death, Jesus or the devil, light or darkness, faith or fear, forgiveness or judgment, heaven or hell, and yes, humility or pride. The choice is yours. But remember, to not choose Christ is to choose against God. A nondecision is a decision in the eyes of God.

Joshua 24:14, "Now therefore fear the Lord, and serve Him in sincerity and in truth: and put away the gods which your fathers served on the other side of the flood, and in Egypt; and serve ye the Lord."

Joshua 24:15, "And is it seem evil unto you to serve the Lord, choose you this day whom ye will serve; whether the gods which your fathers served that were on the other side of the flood, or the gods of the Amorites, in whose land ye dwell: but as for me and my house, we will serve the Lord."

Salvation is believing, receiving, and confessing. Spiritual growth is leaving your old sins and cleaving to Jesus Christ as your total source.

Your heavenly Father, your Creator, is ready to take control of your life, to watch over you, to protect you, and to provide for your every need. God the Father is ready to write your name down in the Book of Life. God the Father is ready for you to repent to God the Son, and then God the Holy Spirit will come into your life. Not three separate Gods, but three different functions in one great God. That's the beauty of it all; God became man, Jesus, and dwelt among us.

Yes, the greatest love story ever told will instantly become a reality in your life. That little babe born in Bethlehem, crucified and resurrected in Jerusalem will be your own personal, eternal Savior this very day.

By simply praying the following prayer, or a similar prayer in your own words, saying it in your heart, you will be saved, born again, redeemed, made new, and will become a Christian.

If you have never been born again, make the decision now to accept Christ. If you once knew the Lord, but fell away into sin, come back to Jesus today, and He will abundantly pardon your sin.

Let's pray together right now and receive the assurance of eternal salvation:

Dear heavenly Father,

I come to you in the name of Jesus who died for my sins and rose again. By His blood, I ask You to wash all my sins away. I renounce my old, sinful life. Forgive me of every sin I've ever committed against others, and forgive me Lord for hurting you.

Dear Jesus, forgive me for my rebellion and pride. I humble myself before You. I know I can't save myself. Please save me Lord, even now, as I call upon Your name. Take away all my sins, fears, and doubts. I trust you right now to save me and to come into my life by Your Holy Spirit. I confess with my mouth that I am a Christian and I've been saved by Your grace. Thank you, Jesus, for letting me be born again and giving me a place in heaven. I will serve You all the days of my life.

Now, Jesus, I give You my problems and talents. Help me Lord, in solving my problems, for I truly believe You live in me, and my problem is Your problem. Give me wisdom Jesus, and let me experience Your peace that passes all understanding.

And Dear Jesus, take my talents and abilities and use them for Your glory. Lead me to a good Bible-believing church and help me to grow in You. And Jesus, give me the privilege of telling others of Your saving grace.

I love You, Jesus. I invite You now, Lord, to love me forever, each day, each minute, in Jesus' name. Amen.

Now, if you prayed the above prayer, you have made a decision for Christ. Remember this is the greatest day of your life. You have just been born again. And, "Who gets to go to heaven?"... You do!

Epilogue

We have launched a national petition that we plan to deliver to our beloved president, congressional leaders, and various state officials.

The purpose of this petition is to encourage each leader to publicly acknowledge the name of Jesus Christ. Without Jesus, our nation will not survive. The following petition is on www.wincityonline.org. Please feel free to copy it, sign it, and pass it on to friends. Please mail it to:

P.O. Box 40, Largo, FL 33779

For more information you can call 1-888-30-JESUS or 1-877-WIN-CITY.

After we receive a substantial amount of signatures, we plan to personally make sure that our beloved president and the members of Congress receive the petitions. Thank you and God bless your efforts and may America say "Jesus!"

Petition
America Say Jesus!

We the undersigned acknowledge that Jesus Christ is Lord "the creator of all things visible and invisible" (Col 1:16, Rev 4:11, Eph 3:9). That God the Father "hath in these last days spoken unto us by His Son, whom he has appointed heir of all things, by whom also he made the worlds" (Heb. 1:2). We believe that Jesus is the Way, the Truth, and the Life and no man goeth unto the Father but by Him (John 14:6). We also hold to the truth that there is "no other name given among men whereby we must be saved (Acts 4:12) that at "the name of Jesus every knee shall bow of things in heaven, and things in earth, and things under the earth; and every tongue confess that Jesus Christ is Lord, to the glory of the Father" (Phil. 2:10-11).

Therefore, we conclude that the name of Jesus must be lifted up and His name proclaimed as the only Redeemer of mankind. We therefore commit our lives to Christ and to the biblical teaching of speaking His Name (Acts 3-5) with boldness and compassion (Acts 4:29-33, 5:40-42). We also commit our lives to the honoring of His name, for Jesus Christ deserves more honor than any name, including Moses (Heb. 3:3). "For He who hath built the house hath more honor than the house itself" (Heb 3:3).

We therefore want to encourage and exhort our beloved President George W. Bush and our wonderful Congress whom we pray for daily, to publicly proclaim and to publicly acknowledge the name and person of Jesus Christ. Our nation is facing many dangers within and from without. We must have God's protection and His blessings. If we truly expect God to protect our nation, we must honor His Son Jesus Christ.

"This Jesus hath God raised up, whereof we all are witnesses" (Acts 2:32).

"And daily in the Temple and in every house they ceased not to teach and preach Jesus Christ"(Acts 5:42).

Name	Address	Phone

An Open Letter to Our President

First of all, let me say how much I respect you, your family, and the office of the presidency. I know you must have enormous pressure, and the many decisions you make affect the entire world. My family and I pray for you and we thank God that He selected you to be our president.

Second, I can surely appreciate the way our political system works. Every vote counts and no politician wants to offend their constituency. However, I believe you can say "Jesus" in such a way that it would not offend most and would please God to pour out even greater blessings on you, your family, and the nation.

Since so many presidents before you have publicly acknowledged Christ, why not continue in their steps? Forget for a moment the anti-Christ crowd and political correctness and think of your heavenly reward. God will extremely bless you for honoring His Son. I'm sorry you have advisors who tell you not to mention Jesus or Christ in your statements. The popular buzz-words seem to be God, religion, or faith. I notice now that your opposing political party is using the same term, faith. It sounds like America needs to honor all gods at the expense of the one true God who has blessed this nation—Jesus Christ.

A few months ago, the media in Europe asked you if Christianity served the same god as the Islamic faith. I know you tried hard not to offend the Muslims or the Christians, but your answer offended both.

Islam cannot be compared to Christianity. A religion that mocks Jews and ridicules the Christian faith should never be called a great or peaceful religion. The Islam religion blasphemes the cross and claims that Jesus Christ never died and was never resurrected. It's sad, but over three hundred Christians are martyred each day at the hands of Muslims.

Mr. President, let me encourage you to acknowledge your personal faith in Christ before sinners. I appreciate the testimony you have given before Christian groups, but the unbelieving world also needs to hear you honor Christ.

Jesus said, "If you confess me before men, I will confess you before my heavenly Father and before his holy angels. But if you deny me before men, I will also deny you before my Father and before His holy angels" (see Matthew 10:32-33).

Jesus continued, "If you are ashamed of me in this sinful and adulterous generation, I will be ashamed of you when I go to my Father which is in heaven."

I'm sure as a believer in Christ, you already know what I'm saying is the truth. However, how can you and every other believer in Christ execute this truth?

If you would oblige me for a moment to give you a suggestion, you can make a statement like this:

"As President of the United States, I am the president for all the people regardless of their religion. I will defend your right to choose your own religion and to worship the god of your choice.

Because I personally believe in Jesus Christ, and because I follow the teachings of the gospel, it is imperative that I love everyone and give to all people the respect that they deserve.

Because America was founded on Christian principles, we are a giving nation and a leader of human rights throughout the world.

My Christianity motivates me to help AIDS victims and to help the less fortunate of the world."

Yes, I'm sure such comments would rile up the liberal media, but it would also move God to protect our nation and our troops. God would protect your integrity and would send a spiritual awakening to our country.

Finally, let me add how much we love and appreciate you and your family. We back you, we support you, and we defend you. Without a doubt, God has chosen you for this hour.

Sincerely in Christ,
David Allbritton

Red Rock Energy Partners, Ltd.

Don Griffin, Mike Nelson, and Josh Nelson

Pastor Bert and Jean Allbritton have pastored some of America's greatest churches. They were founders of First Family church of Dallas, TX. During that pastorate, First Family grew from 29 people to 4000 members.

April is our daughter. She has already ministered in song in 30 countries of the world.

Mike and Anita Nelson. Their love for Christ and each other is a tremendous testimony.

Bob and Lorenda Holden with the Allbrittons. The Holdens are close friends with the Allbrittons and partner in their ministry.

Mildred Rhem has become a close friend of the Allbritton family. She helped make possible the National Jesus Caravan. Many souls are in the Kingdom of God because of Mildred's vision.

Arthur and Denise Blessitt have walked this 12-foot cross into every country of the world. Arthur also had the joy of leading President George W. Bush to the saving knowledge of Jesus Christ. Their cross walk is recorded in the Guinness Book of World Records.

David Allbritton with good friends, Rick and Linda Gigowski. This photo was taken in Ethiopia where Pastor David saw over 1 million salvations for Jesus Christ.

Acknowledgments

I want to personally thank our good friends at Red Rock Energy for their prayerful support and for helping us to get this book throughout America.

Our dear friends, Mike and Anita Nelson, believe in putting Christ first in their lives and in their business.

We recently had Mike Nelson and his partner Dan Griffin to speak at America's Church. They both were anointed of the Holy Spirit, scripturally sound, and enthusiastic about Jesus Christ. They did an incredible job explaining biblical prosperity in conjunction with tithes and offerings. They challenged our business people to be liberal givers into the local church. Mike Nelson's message on Sunday morning was the highlight of the week. His message was so timely and brought tremendous change in our congregation's perception regarding giving. The Holy Spirit moved in a powerful way and God used the service to move our church to another level in Christ.

Their oil and gas company is being used by God to help finance the end time harvest. Their main goal in life is to produce income for the kingdom of God. As a pastor and as a businessman, I highly recommend these anointed men to any church or pastor. Their company and their personal lives are driven by integrity and their desire to help men of God fulfill their God-given destination.

I also highly recommend their business, Red Rock Energy Partners, Ltd. as an incredible investment opportunity. God is blessing them in a very unique way and their financial gain is amazing. As a businessman or businesswoman, you may want to prayerfully consider investing in some of their wells. I can't guarantee absolute success, but from everything I know, Red Rock looks to be a top-notch investment opportunity. And a great bonus is the fact that you would be partnering with Spirit filled Christians.

If you wish to contact Mike Nelson and Dan Griffin you can contact them at:

Phone: (940) 455-7444
E-mail them at mnelson@redrockenergy.com
or write to them at: 2652 FM 407, Suite 250
Bartonville, Texas 76226

For more information about their business and ministry you can log onto: www.redrockenergy.com

Thank you and may God bless you richly,
David Allbritton

Further Information About Red Rock Energy Partners, Ltd.

Red Rock Energy Partners, Ltd. was formed in October of 2001 by Mike Nelson and Dan Griffin. An opportunity arose to purchase an acreage position in Desoto Parish, Louisiana, in which Horizontal James Lime wells could be drilled. The principals had been involved in the drilling of twenty-two similar wells in Shelby County, Texas. The Shelby County wells had been enormously successful; therefore when the opportunity presented itself, it was a natural progression.

Red Rock began by successfully drilling seven horizontal James Lime wells in Desoto Parish as a non-operator. Then the company undertook development of a new field in Shelby County, Texas. Red Rock has drilled two wells there down to the Travis Peak formation and discovered the James Lime as well as several other potentially productive formations. The company has currently put together over four thousand acres in Shelby County, Texas, with plans to continue its James Lime Horizontal programs. So far, Red Rock has successfully drilled and is producing from one horizontal James Lime well in Shelby County. The company believes that a new potential field discovery is now in the making. Nine wells are currently producing, and one is still under completion.

The company has assembled a team of people both in-house and from a consulting position to drill, complete, and operate wells proficiently in East Texas. Our experience and success bodes well for potential partners and inventors who share a desire to invest in oil and gas at the wellhead.

Red Rock Energy Team:

Mike Nelson, oversees the field operations and prospect evaluations. Mr. Nelson has over twenty years of experience in the oil and gas industry as an operator, exploration and production entrepreneur, marketing, fund raising, buying and selling of properties, mineral and royalty buying and selling, and pretty much anything related. Mr. Nelson has an abundance of contacts within the industry.

Dan Griffin, oversees the administrative side of the business including but not limited to legal, accounting, bank and finance, and investor relations. Mr. Griffin entered the oil and gas arena in 2000 and co-founded Red Rock Energy Partners, Ltd. along with Mr. Nelson in 2001.

Dale Gentry, serves as company chaplain. Mr. Gentry is as international voice to the church and currently serves as pastor of Gateway Church International.

Special Thanks

I want to thank my daughter, April (sixteen), for her outstanding work in the typing and the editing of this book. Her straight A's in school finally paid off. She is a delight and I'm confident April will be used of God mightily throughout the world (all boys calling for dates must be sold out for Jesus). However, I first expect her to average a triple double this year in basketball. How about an average of twenty points, eighteen rebounds and fourteen blocks—that should get her a basketball scholarship and save her mom and dad some money.

I also want to thank Andrew and Matthew (fifteen), my powerful twin boys. Andrew is being groomed to be President of the United States, and Matthew wants to make millions playing pro basketball. (I hope they all tithe!) As you can tell, we love humor in our house!

Seriously, my children are such a blessing to Linda and I. They all love Jesus, and each one is a strong witness for Christ. I also want to thank my dear wife Linda for our twenty-six years of marriage. I love her so much. God gave me such a beautiful person and a wonderful companion. We enjoy living for Jesus together.

I also want to thank my parents, Bert and Jean Allbritton for their love, friendship, and continued support. Dad is still the greatest Preacher on earth, and my wife agrees, no one can cook like my mom!

Also, with a deep heart of gratitude, I want to thank my sister, Sharon Axton, for her preliminary typing of this manuscript, and to Bob Penello for his expertise in editing. I also deeply appreciate the insight from my attorney, Thaddeus Freeman and the wonderful business that he and his lovely wife Jan operate for the glory of God.

Linda and I also deeply appreciate her brother, Tim Carelock, who has continued to help our ministry in so many ways. Tim is not only my brother-in-law, but also a dear friend.

Through the years, Linda and I have developed a close friendship with Arthur and Denise Blessitt. Their heart for God and their continued encouragement has lifted our spirits. Their cross walk continues to reach multitudes throughout the world.

Plus, we can never forget our dear friends, Rick and Linda Gigowski, who have been missionary comrades with us throughout the world, and our longtime friends, Gary and Sheree Sutton. Their business success is a constant reminder of God's faithfulness!

P.S. I would also like to thank the principal, Mr. Cathey, and the faculty of Calvary Christian High School for giving our children an awesome education. This high school in Clearwater is one of the top academic schools in the country. It's also one of the upcoming great athletic schools. Our children are really excited to be in their basketball program under the athletic direction of the men's basketball coach, Dave Bintz and the girl's coach, Shane Krotz.

Further Thanks

For the past year or so, Linda and I have had to believe God for supernatural finances. We also needed some close friends. Besides all of our dear friends at America's Church, there were a few people that spent hours each week praying for us, encouraging us, and standing with us for financial miracles. Besides the names already mentioned, I want to thank Mildred Rehm, Thaddeus and Jan Freeman, and Bob and Lorenda Holden. Their friendship and prayers have made a huge impact on our lives. They all helped Linda and I to keep laughing and to keep on believing God for miracles! (And Bob is the best joke teller in America). Laughter has been such a blessing!

Also for the continued friendship and financial help of Pastor Jon and Toni Ogle of First Family Church, Sharon and Ron Axton, Kimberly Jett, and of course the greatest parents on earth, Bert and Jean Allbritton.

Furthermore, the years of friendship with Pastor Terry and Carol Kirk and the ongoing friendship with Larry and Shirley Turner have blessed Linda and I immensely. We've shared a lot of laughs and tears together. Thank God for all of our friends.

We want to thank the following wonderful people who work so hard for this ministry: Patsy Kaleel, Arlene Varrati, Lynn Lemarr, and to our wonderful staff, Clay and Jessica Runnels, Bob and Kristin Penello and Jason and Tricia Glasgow.

We would like to dedicate this book to the following people that are special to us:

Mike and Anita Nelson	James and Judith Rundle
Bob and Lorenda Holden	Brenda Fleming
Thaddeus and Jan Freeman	Curt and Alicia Slatton
Mildred Rehm	Jay and Gloria Hamilton
Bert and Jean Allbritton	Joe and Julie Martinez
Ron and Sharon Axton, Kim Jett	Herb Gonzalez
Tami and Greg Napier	Rick Henningsen

Linda's Family: Betty Carelock
Tim Carelock and Zac,
Doyle and Nina Carelock
Roger and Carla Carelock
Rick and Linda Gigowski
Gary and Sheree Sutton
Jon and Toni Ogle
Arthur and Denise Blessitt
Larry and Shirley Turner
Cord and Donna Blankenship
Terry and Carol Kirk
Gary and Ro Lashua
Ed and Patsy Kaleel
Chip Schneider
Linda Brewer
Kelly and Kylie Lance
Karen Berry
Gary Wetendorf
Catherine Misher
David and Gloria Baacke
Jonathan Newhall
David and Gloria Baacke
Alex and Amy Fasy
Joe and Treva Brown
Louise Ward
Tammie Christian
Vernie Sanger
Vergie Mahoney
Jackie Morris
Lillie Wills
Robert McIntyre
Mary Edmiston
Melissa Bonacci
Helen Severs

Gary Miller
Theo and Bev Wolmarins
Dennis and Nettie Holt
Rick and Carol Lamb
Lyle and Pamela Houpt
Jim and Julie Baker
Allen and Faith Gourley
Milt and Rose Covert
J. and Dorothy Foster
David and Theresa Pittman
Jim and Janell Moore
Elizabeth Parrish
Denise Mock
Keith Roadarmer
Wayne and Adrienne Ritchie
Jerry and Barbara Reeves
Virginia Crawford
Russ and Suzan Kenaston
Robert and Joan Kling
Rosemarie Roussel
Daniel and Virginia Joseph
Henry and Deloris Clark
Mary Koplinski
Mike and Monica Henson
Gwen Grubb
Veronica Fuller
Mr. and Mrs. Mike Norris-
of Fast Signs
Randy Eyerman
Vicki Morahan
Steve Washinko, Jr.
Judy Hatch
Kay Bonacci

The following pastors and ministers have been a tremendous blessing to this evangelistic ministry. They have personally ministered to Linda and I, and have exhorted us to do great things for

God. May the Lord's very best always be upon them, their families, and ministries:

Pastor Tommy Barnett

Pastor Jon & Toni Ogle

Pastor Dan Sheaffer

Pastor Bob & Joy Nichols

Pastor Theo & Bev Wolmarans

Pastor Ann & John Giminez

Pastor Terry Whitley

Pastor Gloria Gillespie

Pastor Danny & Dena Smith

Pastor Tony Cribb

Pastor Jerry & Sandy Bernard

Pastor J.B. Whitfield

Pastor Ray & Becky Larson

Pastor Phil Morocco

Dr. Jim Morocco

Pastor Robb & Linda Thompson

Pastor Terry & Carol Kirk

Pastor Donald & Nora Fozard

Pastor Rich & Phyllis Callahan

Pastor Earnest Fry

Pastor Al & Tara Brice

Pastor Steve & Gil Barry

Pastor Leonard Gardner

Pastor Matt & Debra Metlott

Pastor Keith Johnson

Pastor Gary Greenwald

Pastor Mel Mullen

Pastor Mike & Kathy Hayes

Pastor Merv Walker

Pastor Gwen & Norma Turner

Pastor Orville & Carolyn Phillips

Pastor Allan & Janine Bagg

Pastor Wayne & Monica Cochran

Pastor Rose King

Pastor Reggie & Sadie Vinson

Pastor David Katina

America's Church

Linda and I had the privilege of starting America's Church in Largo, Florida. Even though the church is just over one year old, God has given us many outstanding miracles.

From the inception and birth of the church, souls have been saved, healed, and delivered by the power of God. The name of Jesus has changed countless lives, and many have been filled with the Holy Spirit.

Our church is filled with Pentecostals, Baptists, Catholics, and many new converts. The Lord has also sent us many talented workers and an incredible staff.

Even though I have evangelized throughout America and overseas, the church has continued to grow and has impacted our city.

We believe the future is bright. We give God all the glory for everything He has done. Jesus is changing lives!

Thank You, Jesus, for these wonderful pastors who are leading our nation to a great spiritual Awakening:

Pastor Jon & Toni Ogle
First Family Church
Dallas, Texas

Dr. Jon Ogle is an anointed man of God who honors Jesus Christ. Jon and Toni have been faithful ministers of the gospel for over twenty years. They pastored a great church in Roswell, New Mexico and were also the Presidents of Gateway Christian School.

Today they pastor one of America's most exciting churches: First Family Church of Dallas, Texas. They followed the founding pastors, Bert and Jean Allbritton, and have continued the great Bible tradition at First Family.

Under the anointed leadership of Pastor Ogle, First Family Church has grown both numerically and spiritually. Pastor Jon and Toni are on the cutting edge of charismatic thought and doctrine.

Pastor Jon moves in the gifts of the Holy Spirit and is a very anointed speaker. First Family Church is a Pentecostal, soul winning church. It's dynamic worship and praise band presents some of the most anointed music in America. Today, First Family Church has an excess of four thousand members.

Pastor Cord and Donna Blankenship
Refiners Fire
Ennis, Texas

Pastor Cord and Donna Blankenship have an on-fire Pentecostal church in Ennis, Texas. Refiners Fire is a life-changing church. People are being delivered from drugs, alcoholism, and other vices of Satan.

The personal testimonies of Pastors Cord and Donna are absolutely incredible. The grace of God and the power of the Holy Spirit changed their lives forever.

Refiners Fire is changing the city of Ennis. Pastor Cord and Donna's church is packed out each Sunday morning and is looking to expand their present facility.

Pastor Cord is also involved with the city and is a voice of righteousness in the political realm. God is blessing Refiners Fire because of their heart for God.

Pastor Dean and Kathy Shropshire
Choose Life Victory Center
Hobbs, New Mexico

Pastor and Mrs. Dean Shropshire pastor an incredible, anointed church in Hobbs, New Mexico. Their church is growing both numerically and spiritually. They have dynamic teachings of God's word and an awesome band and worship team.

Pastor Shropshire has a vision to win his city to Christ and to impact the United States. Both he and his wife are spirit filled pastors and emphasize walking by faith. Their church is a beautiful blend of charismatic worship with Pentecostal power.

To drive up to their church, one is moved by the size of the crowd, but more so by the people's enthusiasm for Christ.

This is a Bible-believing, soul winning church that is turning its city to Christ.

Recommended Resource Reading

Graham, Frank, *The Name,* Nashville, Tn. Thomas Nelson, Inc. 2002

Arthur S. Demoss Foundation, *The Rebirth of America,* Philadelphia, Penn. 1986

Black, Jim Nelson, *America Adrift,* Fort Lauderdale, Fl. Coral Ridge Ministry 2002

Limbaugh, David, *Persecution,* Washington, D.C. Regnery Publishing, Inc. 2003

La Haye, Tim, *Why Believe in Jesus,* Eugene, Ore. Harvest House Publishers, 2004

Allbritton, David, *Answers To Life's Most Complicated Questions,* Dallas, TX. The David L. Allbritton Finally Free World Outreach, Inc. 2001

Allbritton, David, *The Father's Business,* Dallas TX. The David L. Allbritton Finally Free World Outreach, Inc. 1991

Allbritton, David, *Heaven, Who Gets To Go,* Dallas, TX. The David L. Allbritton Finally Free World Outreach, Inc. 1982

JerryFalwell.com, *"What American Presidents said about the Bible"* Retrieved on July 15, 2004

Books and Manuscripts by David Allbritton

- More than Just Friends
- The Father's Business
- Heaven, Who Gets to Go?
- Please Let Me Preach
- Get Your Hopes Up
- Answers to Life's Most Complicated Questions
- My G & B Goals
- Welcome to Your New Life
- Nobody Will Ever Love You As Much As I Do
- Desert Storms Spiritual Warfare
- One on One
- Yes, You Can Win Souls
- The Steps of a Good Man
- Finally Free Forever
- To the People of Scotland
- You can Keep It
- We Celebrate Your Decision For Christ
- Your Dreams Are On Their Way
- I Can Win Your City to Christ in One Month
- The Truth About Terrorism
- Excitement in Life
- 120 Reasons I am a Soul Winner
- God's Going to Give You a Break
- Make a Miracle Happen
- Step By Step
- Around the World with Jesus
- God Bless You and Your Family!
- A Message to Your Unsaved Loved Ones
- America Say Jesus!

Author Contact Information

David Allbritton Ministries
P.O. Box 40
Largo, FL 33779
727-538-3011 or 1-888-30-JESUS
E-mail address: wincity@wincityonline.org
Web sites: www.wincityonline.org
and www.americasayjesus.com

Endorsements of David Allbritton's Ministry

James Robinson writes, "David Allbritton is a gifted and undeniably anointed evangelist. He will reach the lost and stimulate Christians to win souls to Christ."

"When he leaves a city, many will have come to Christ, believers will be filled with the Spirit and many will become fruitful witnesses. What a difference this makes in a church or community. As a man of faith, this is the difference that really counts."

"Let me hasten to add that David and Linda are a wonderful, consistent Christian couple; and these days, integrity and consistency are so vitally important. David and his family will honor the Lord and bless people wherever they go to minister the Word. I am thrilled to be associated with him and to be his friend."

Pastor Tommy Barnett writes about David Allbritton: "Your ministry was so special. People were really touched. I sure understand why you have risen so far; it is so evident because of your great heart and character and passion for the lost and hurting. You were awesome! People are still talking about your great message. You will never know how much you have encouraged me. May God richly bless you, your family and ministry."

"David Allbritton is one of the best teachers of soul winning anywhere. He presents the Gospel with sincerity, clarity and boldness with grace."

"From creative outreach ideas to an instant in-season witness, David is indeed one of the greatest personal soul winners I have ever known. Every person who comes across his path is blessed by his dedication and love for souls."

Pastor Bob Nichols writes, "David's preaching is a beautiful combination of anointed zeal, yet a compassion and tenderness for souls that is so needed today. His sincerity and effectiveness as a soul winner got my attention. He wins souls from the pulpit and also personally. David is an experienced, anointed evangelist who has preached in some of the best-known churches, auditoriums, and stadiums of our day. David's preaching and Linda's beautiful singing will bless any church and pastor who truly desires to win souls and reach their city for Jesus."

International Author, Speaker, and Church Growth Expert, Winkey Pratney writes, "It has been my privilege to meet and get to know David Allbritton and his lovely family. David has an unusual touch from God in the area of personal evangelism and is one of the most radical men I have ever met in more than thirty years of outreach in the field of witnessing. He is also an excellent preacher and communicator, one of the few ministries whose tapes I wanted to take home and play to my family."

Pastor Terry Kirk of Central Christian Assembly in Baltimore, Maryland writes, "It gives me pleasure to recommend the ministry of David Allbritton. Since our crusade with David, in just two months, our attendance has increased by approximately one hundred people. A large number of these are a result of individuals reaching out to the lost. Rev. Allbritton challenged our people to church growth via soul winning and discipleship. He also took public pledges to do so. As a result, our people pledged to pass out 148,000 tracts, to invite over 13,000 people to church and to pray for the Lord's harvest. We are continually hearing testimonies of the Lord's daily ministry in our lives.

"I have known many men who are in the ministry of evangelism, but few have the ministry of evangelist. David is a walking, living soul winner whose message is not only for the lost, but greatly stirred the desire of believers to renew themselves again with their first love experience with Christ."

"If you are wanting to see the renewal of the Holy Ghost and have a desire for the ministry of evangelism burst forth again in your people, then I highly recommend the ministry of David Allbritton."

Pastor Mike Linney of Bethel Temple of Lafayette, Louisiana writes, "David Allbritton is recognized as one of America's greatest soul winning evangelists and motivators in the Body of Christ. In a recent meeting in our Church, the congregation pledged to pass out 9,630 tracts a week and to invite over 14,400 people to our church. This will reach our city in four months with the gospel. Brother David preaches a strong word and is outstanding in getting people saved in the actual revival service. Every service people filled the altar for salvation and rededication. I've never had a revival when so many people came to Christ. David has authored a variety of books and has appeared on numerous TV programs (700 Club, Praise the Lord and others) across America and overseas. He has a hunger for revival and helping the local church grow and flourish. God is granting his heart's desire."

Notes